T0128247

DANIEL'S
SEVENTIETH
WEEK

The Final Seven Years Before Eternity

RONALD F. GREEN

WESTBOW
PRESS®
A DIVISION OF THOMAS NELSON
& ZONDERVAN

WestBow Press books may be ordered through booksellers or by contacting:

WestBow Press
A Division of Thomas Nelson & Zondervan
1663 Liberty Drive
Bloomington, IN 47403
www.westbowpress.com
1 (866) 928-1240

All Scripture listed is from the **Authorized Version** or **King James Version** (**KJV**), 1611, 1769.Outside of the United Kingdom, the KJV is in the public domain. Within the United Kingdom, the rights to the KJV are vested in the Crown.

ISBN: 978-1-9736-3165-1 (sc)
ISBN: 978-1-9736-3166-8 (hc)
ISBN: 978-1-9736-3164-4 (e)

Library of Congress Control Number: 2018907210

Print information available on the last page.

WestBow Press rev. date: 07/20/2018

DEDICATION

To my wife Sharon:

Sharon, in Proverbs 31 God tells us that to find a virtuous woman is a good thing. God has blessed me with a wife that meets all the requirements of Proverbs 31 for a virtuous woman. Over the years you have encouraged me in my walk with God and to use the spiritual gifts that God has given me. You have proofread this work, corrected my grammar and spelling. Even after all these years you are still putting your hands to the spindle to aid me in my ministry.

To Dr. Dan Dickerson:

Pastor Dan, you have always made yourself available to meet with me for advice. You have always encouraged me to keep on with my study of Scripture, to keep following the LORD, and to use the spiritual gifts that God has given me.

My brother in Christ, Ken Shelley Jr.:

Ken, you have always encouraged me when I needed to discuss this prophecy. You would always have a ready Scripture and a suggestion on how I might want to consider rephrasing a sentence to make it more understandable to the readers so that they would have a better understanding of the truths found in God's Word.

CONTENTS

Author's Note:
Salvation

At the beginning of this work that God has given me to do, I feel I must start with the most important event in your life: your own personal salvation. To understand the events that we are about to experience in this world, you must first agree with certain truths. The first is that there is a God. God is holy. As such, He cannot allow sin into His heaven. The apostle Paul, writing to the Romans, says,

> "For all have sinned and come short of the glory of God"
> (Rom. 3:23)

"All" means me, you, your parents, and everyone that has ever existed or will exist on this planet. It includes any preacher, seminary professor, priest, pope, or leader of any denomination or religion. The *only* exception is the Lord Jesus Christ, who was born of a virgin, lived His entire life without sin, and laid His life down to redeem us, that we might be forgiven for our sins and live for eternity.

Jesus Christ was born of a woman and therefore was 100 percent human. As a human, He got tired and hungry. He bled if He got cut. However, since His Father was God, He was also 100 percent God. This gave Him a unique dual nature. As a human, He slept in a boat during a storm. This terrified His disciples, since they felt that they were about to die. As God, when He was awakened, He spoke a word and the storm ended. As a human, when Christ heard that His friend Lazarus had died, He wept at the tomb. As God, in the next breath, He called for Lazarus to come forth, and a man who had been dead for four days came out of the grave. God considers sin so bad that He has declared that the penalty for it is death:

> "For the wages of sin is death; but the gift of God is eternal life through Jesus Christ our Lord." (Rom. 6:23)

Though God has declared this penalty for sin, He does not want any person to be punished for it, due to His love for us. Please understand that hell was created for Satan and his demons. At the final judgment, Satan and his followers will be cast into the lake of fire for eternity, but God has provided us a way to be forgiven.

> "For God so loved the world, that he gave his only begotten Son, that whosoever believeth in him should not perish, but have everlasting life. (John 3:16)

> For God sent not his Son into the world to condemn the world; but that the world through him might be saved. (John 3:17)

> He that believeth on him is not condemned: but he that believeth not is condemned already, because he hath not believed in the name of the only begotten Son of God. (John 3:18)

> Jesus saith unto him, I am the way, the truth, and the life: no man cometh unto the Father, but by me. (John 14:6)

> That if thou shalt confess with thy mouth the Lord Jesus, and shalt believe in thine heart that God hath raised him from the dead, thou shalt be saved. For with the heart man believeth unto righteousness; and with the mouth confession is made unto salvation. For the scripture saith, whosoever believeth on him shall not be ashamed. For there is no difference between the Jew and the Greek: for the same Lord over all is rich unto all that call upon him.

For whosoever shall call upon the name of the Lord shall be saved. (Rom. 10:9–13)

Behold, I stand at the door, and knock: if any man hear my voice, and open the door, I will come in to him, and will sup with him, and he with me. To him that overcometh will I grant to sit with me in my throne, even as I also overcame, and am set down with my Father in his throne." (Rev. 3:20–21)

It is also made clear that there is no other way to be saved. Luke tells us,

"Neither is there salvation in any other: for there is none other name under heaven given among men, whereby we must be saved". (Acts 4:12)

Salvation has been made quite simple. You do not need someone to say a prayer for you. In fact, a prayer said by someone else will not do you any good. You need to repent (have a change of heart and have a desire to live for God), ask the Lord to forgive you, and receive Him into your heart. The repentance must be sincere. We are told in very plain language that receiving Jesus Christ as Lord is the *only* way to be saved. Placing your trust in Muhammad, Buddha, or any other proclaimed prophet will only get you an eternity in hell.

If you are trusting in having been baptized as an infant, then you are currently lost. If you claim that you received Christ as a very young child, you may want to make sure of your salvation now that you are older. We know from Scripture that a child who has not reached the age of accountability is not guilty, but once you reach the age of accountability, you are held to the judgment of Christ.

The second truth to agree on is that God created man as being eternal. When we leave this life, we will continue to live for eternity. Where we spend eternity is our choice. We can either live for eternity with God by accepting His gift or spend eternity in hell by rejecting His gift. Ten days after Christ ascended into heaven, the day of Pentecost arrived, and the

Holy Spirit was poured out. The message Peter preached that day gave the plan for us to have eternal life. In Acts 2:38 when Peter was asked by the Jews that were present as to what they had to do to receive eternal life, Peter said the following:

> "Then Peter said unto them, Repent, and be baptized every one of you in the name of Jesus Christ for the remission of sins, and ye shall receive the gift of the Holy Ghost. (Acts 2:38)

> For the promise is unto you, and to your children, and to all that are afar off, *even* as many as the Lord our God shall call." (Acts 2:39)

By rejecting God's gift of eternal life, you will spend eternity in the lake of fire prepared for Satan and his angels. It will be your choice and I pray that if you have not accepted Christ into your heart, you do so now. If God should remove the church from this planet prior to you doing so, then you will be eternally lost. Please understand that it is not God who will condemn you to the lake of fire. It will be your choice for refusing to accept the gift of eternal life being offered.

Jewish Calendar

Day: When God created everything, He proclaimed the evening and the morning as a day. A day, as defined in Scripture, is *always* the time from evening to evening or sunset to sunset. In our world, we change our day at midnight. The Jewish calendar, on the other hand, makes the change from one day to the next at sunset. Jews still use the setting of the sun as the moment to switch from one day to the next. For the dates on the calendar pages that follow, remember that the day started at sunset the previous date. The Jewish calendar does not use names for days. Days are numbered one through seven.

Lunar Month: A month on the Jewish calendar is a lunar month of 29 days, 12 hours, 44 minutes, and 2.8 seconds, or 29.53059 days. This is also known as the monthly synodic cycle, the length of time it takes for the moon to return to the exact position, relative to the earth, as it was when initially measured.

The new moon, which marks the start of every Jewish month, is the most pivotal date in the Jewish calendar. Without the new moon, there would not be any Jewish holidays. All the Jewish holidays revolve around the date of the new moon.

Months in the Jewish calendar start with the crescent of the moon *after* what is called the dark of the moon. Every month, the moon reaches a day when there is no reflectance of light from its surface. This is called a new moon or the dark of the moon. The next day at sunset, a very thin crescent is visible (see images below) for up to ninety minutes after the sun sets. To see the crescent, you must be looking directly at where the sun has set. This is what is known in Hebrew as the Rishon or first of the month. On the Jewish calendar this day is called Rosh Chodesh or the head of the month.

The crescent moon cannot be seen at any other time on this day, as the moon is within a ten-degree arc of the sun. For the purpose of the Jewish calendar, the crescent moon must be visible to the naked eye before it sets *in Jerusalem*. Jews celebrate the first day of the month, the new moon or Rosh Chodesh, as a minor holiday.

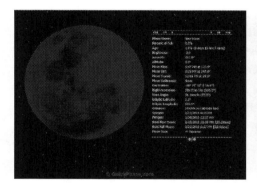

January 13, 2021, at sunset
at Jerusalem, Israel
(Dark of the moon)

January 14, 2021, at sunset
at Jerusalem, Israel
(Crescent of the moon)

In these two images, the dark of the moon will occur at sunset on January 13, 2021, the next to last day of Tevet (Tevet 28, 5781). The day became Tevet 29 at sunset, and the daylight part of Tevet 29 will occur on January 14, 2021. At sunset, a crescent moon will be seen. At that moment, it will become the next day and, in this case, the next month: Sh'vat 1, 5781.

When the Jews had the Sanhedrin and the temple, the phase of the moon was determined by two witnesses who reported when they had seen the crescent moon. The Sanhedrin asked the witnesses a few simple questions to determine if they really had seen the crescent or were lying about it. The questions went like this:

- Did the sun go down before the moon or did the moon go down before the sun?
- Was the moon to the north of the sun or was it to the south of the sun?
- What direction were the tips of the crescent pointing?
- How high in the sky did the moon appear to be?
- How wide was it?

Anyone would be able to answer these questions if they really had seen the crescent. After the witnesses were questioned, the Sanhedrin (high priest) would verify the sighting and proclaim the new month. After the destruction of the temple, calculations were used to determine when the new moon was visible in Jerusalem. Today we use computerized calculations to set the calendar.

In this book, I have included images that are not available in normal calendars. I show not only the normal monthly calendar, but also the image of the moon for the appropriate month. This allows you to verify the calendar and when the month started based on the moon phase. All moon phases are shown for Jerusalem. The moon *must* be seen in the sky and cannot be below the horizon.

Year: A Jewish year consists of twelve months. Since a month is not always thirty days long, the length of one year will vary. It may be 353, 354, or 355 days long. This variation in length would cause the Jewish months to rotate around the seasons. A month that first occurred in the spring would rotate over the years into the winter, then the fall, and then the summer before eventually falling again in the spring. For this reason, the Jews need to add a "leap month" every so often to realign their calendar with the sun. This is called a *lunisolar calendar* (lunar/solar). The adjustment keeps all of God's days in the time of year when they were originally placed. A year that has a leap month will have 383, 384, or 385 days.

I have provided a chart showing you the Jewish months as well as the number of days in each month. You will also see that with each month, I have included what the moon will look like on each day of the month. I hope this will help you to understand the calendar.

Jewish Calendar Month Names

English	Month Number	Length	Gregorian Calendar Equivalent
Nissan	1	30 days	March–April
Lyyar	2	29 days	April–May
Sivan	3	30 days	May–June
Tamuz	4	29 days	June–July
Av	5	30 days	July–August
Elul	6	29 days	August–September
Tishri –	7	30 days	September–October
Cheshvan	8	29 or 30 days	October–November
Kislev	9	29 or 30 days	November–December
Tevet	10	29 days	December–January
Sh'vat	11	30 days	January–February
Adar I (leap years only)	12	30 days	February–March
Adar (called Adar II in leap years)	12	29 days	February–March

Julian Day - To determine length of time, scientists use what is called Julian Days. A Julian Day (abbreviated JD) is simply a count of days. This was developed in 1583 and is used mainly by astronomers, and historians to decide length of time between two dates. There are seven thousand nine hundred eighty years in a Julian Day cycle. This is calculated by taking the twenty-eight-year solar cycle (when the Gregorian calendar repeats itself), times the nineteen-year lunar cycle (when the moon phases begin to repeat themselves) times the fifteen-year cycle used by the Roman Empire to decide taxes. The chosen starting date for Julian dates is noon Jan 1, 4713 BC. Universal Time is considered the starting point for a given date. A Julian Day is a whole number to find the difference between dates. The decimal numbers are the determination for one day of twenty-four hours per day, sixty minutes per hour, and sixty seconds per minute. According to astronomers the accuracy of a Julian Day is to within one microsecond (0.99999 seconds). Simply count the number of days from the start of the current cycle to current and future dates. The end of this current Julian Day cycle is January 22, 3268 AD. This allows you to find dates from any point in history to any point in the near future. To figure out the length of time between two dates, you take the largest number and subtract the smaller number giving you the total number of days between the dates. A second use is to determine the date a certain number of days after an initial date. If a start date is unknown but the number of days is known, you determine the Julian Day number for a determined date, subtract the number of days, then determine the date for that Julian Day number. The following website will allow you to access the Julian Day calculator for the U.S. Navy. (http://aa.usno.navy. mil/data/docs/JulianDate.php) The use of "Julian Dates" are used as confirmation for the first sixty-nine weeks of Jesus Christ's first coming and crucifixion in AD 31.

The Feasts or Appointed Times of the Lord

In Leviticus 23, God states that there are seven proclaimed "feasts." The word translated as "feast" in Scripture is the Hebrew word *moed*, which means "appointed time." Of the seven feasts proclaimed, four are in the spring of the year and three in the fall. The spring feasts are Passover, the Feast of Unleavened Bread, the Feast of Firstfruits, and Pentecost or the Feast of Weeks. Feasts must be fulfilled on the actual day of the feast. God proclaims that the "appointed time" is a "holy convocation." In Hebrew, this term is *kodesh mik-raw*, meaning a dress rehearsal for the event that will fulfill the appointed time.

From ancient times to the present, God and His servants, the Jews, have counted the passage of time in units of twelve months per year. God declared in Scripture that a month begins when the new moon crescent can first be seen after the dark of the moon, when no moon is visible. The new moon is the point of no reflectance. As the moon cycles, its reflectance increases until it reaches full moon status with one hundred percent reflectance. From that point, the moon's reflectance decreases to zero again. Zero reflectance is also called "the dark of the moon." If there is only one day in the month when the moon is dark, then it is also considered the new moon. If there are two days that appear dark, then the first day is called the dark of the moon and the second day is called the new moon. The length of the moon cycle has been determined by the scientific community to be twenty-nine days, twelve hours, forty-four minutes, and 2.8 seconds.

God has declared that the start of a month is when the first crescent of the moon is visible after the moon has reached zero percent reflectance. The moon at this point is almost directly in line with the sun as it is setting, so the crescent moon can only be seen for a few minutes after the sun has completely set.

God has likewise determined that a day is to be counted from sunset on one day until the sun sets on the next day. The calendar pages I have shown here are hybrids of the Gregorian and Jewish calendars. The months are listed as we normally see them on our Gregorian calendars. However, the days are counted according to the Jewish method. A given day starts at sunset on the previous day and continues until sunset of the day shown. Since this is a hybrid solar/lunar calendar, Jewish months are also shown. The term "Rosh Chodesh" is applied to the first day of the Jewish month. It means "start" or "head of" the month. This is a reference to when the crescent of the moon is first visible, signifying that the month has changed.

God started the counting of time by saying that the evening and morning constituted a single day of twenty-four hours each. God created the sun and moon and made them the determination for all the timing in His creation:

> "And God said, let there be lights in the firmament of the heaven to divide the day from the night; and let them be for signs, and for seasons, and for days, and years" (Gen. 1:14).

Again, please note that in this verse, the word translated "seasons" does not mean the seasons as we know them in Western culture. It is originally the Hebrew word *moed* and means "appointed times."

Tishri 1

Tishri is the seventh month of the Jewish calendar. The first is also New Year day for the Jews. It is on Tishri 1 that the Jews start their new year, in the same way that January first is the start of the new year in the Gregorian calendar. It is only on this day that Israel will sign a peace agreement.

Tishri 1 starts the Jewish days of repentance, which last until Tishri 10, the Day of Atonement. This day is also called by several other names. One is the Marriage Supper of the Messiah. Christ tells us in Luke 13:18–30 that once God closes the door to this supper, there is no more entrance. Christ tells us in Matthew 25:1–12 that the kingdom of heaven is like ten virgins who went out to meet the bridegroom. Five were wise and five were foolish. The five foolish virgins took lamps but no oil; the five wise virgins took lamps and oil. As the bridegroom tarried, they slept. They awoke when a cry was made that the bridegroom had come. The five foolish virgins had to find more oil for their lamps, while the five wise went in with the bridegroom and "the door was shut." When the five foolish virgins returned, they were told "I do not know you." The door was shut against them.

Once the church is removed from this earth to be with Christ, there will be no second chance to go in. It will be as in the days of Noah: when Noah and his family entered the ark, God shut the door so no one else could enter. Noah was unable to lower the door to let others in. Their eternity was determined in the same way yours will be if you do not accept Christ. Repent and ask Christ to save you before the church is removed. Your eternity is at stake. Please do not reject it.

Titles for Rosh Hashanah

- Rosh Hashanah—Birthday of the World
- Feast of Trumpets—God's Appointed Time (Leviticus 23)
- The Awakening Blast of the Righteous
- The Coronation of the Messiah
- The Marriage Supper of the Messiah
- The Judgment of the Righteous
- The Opening of the Books of Judgment
- The Day that No Man Knows (Matthew 24:36; Mark 13:32)

Rosh Hashanah

According to Jews this is the day that God created the world. This is the reason, according to Jewish practice, that Israel will sign a peace agreement only on this day—for example, the agreement with Jordan and the cease-fire agreement with the Palestinian Authority in 2014. The start of this month also changes the year number that the Jews use for calculating their year.

Feast of Trumpets

This feast is also known as *yom teruah*, the day of sounding the trumpets. Of all of God's appointed times, this is the only one that occurs at the start of the month. During the first century, when the temple and the Sanhedrin existed, the start of a new month could only be determined after two independent witnesses reported to the Sanhedrin that they had seen the new moon. It was only on the start of this day that "no man knows the day or hour of it" (Matt. 24:36; Mark 13:32). When Christ said that, He was using an idiom that His disciples understood. Today we know exactly when that day will start, so we no longer require two witnesses to testify.

The celebration of this day calls for three shofars to be blown. Each shofar has its own unique sound. The shofars are grouped in different ways to produce different sounds, for a total of ninety-nine blasts. After the ninety-ninth blast, another trumpet is sounded, which likewise has its own unique sound. This is known as "the last trump."

This feast is also known as *yom hadin*, or the day of judgment of the righteous. It is on this day that Christ will judge believers at the bema seat. Christians believe that at this time the book of works will be opened, and Christians will be judged on their works. This judgment of works determines the crowns we will receive, not our salvation. The fact that we are there will mean that we are written in the book of life and have taken part in the first resurrection.

★★★

The calendar pages in this book cover the last generation of this age. They go from the signing of an agreement with Israel on Rosh Hashanah 2019 until Yom Kippur seven years later. The single number at the bottom of each day denotes the number of days since the agreement was signed. It counts up to 1,260 days from the signing of the agreement to when the altar will be desecrated.

At that point, two numbers appear at the bottom of each day. The top number is the count of days from the desecration of the altar to the end of the week, which will be 1,290 days as stated by the angel: "And from the time *that* the daily *sacrifice* shall be taken away, and the abomination that makes desolate set up, *there shall be* a thousand two hundred and ninety days" (Dan. 12:11).

The bottom number counts the days starting when the Antichrist receives the full power of Satan until the end of the week and the start of eternity. This is the forty-two months that the Antichrist has the full power of Satan. This count is 1,260 days and will end on Yom Kippur, the Day of Atonement, at the end of the seventieth week. This is also the day that Jesus Christ will return to the Mount of Olives, enter the third temple, and begin His reign of one thousand years.

The last day of this calendar is Yom Kippur. Jesus Christ will return on this day with His armies. He will defeat the Antichrist and false prophet, who will be cast into the lake of fire. Satan himself will be cast into the bottomless pit and locked away for the one thousand years of Christ's reign.

Generations and the
Last Generation

A major discussion over the past two thousand years has been "When does a generation start?" A related question is "How long is a generation?" Misunderstanding surrounds these questions. The misunderstanding occurs because many good men of God have taken a single Scripture passage and used it out of context. When Moses sent twelve spies into the Promised Land, ten of the twelve brought back a report that they were unable to take the land because the people were too big. The spies would not trust in God to do what had been promised. God then declared that the Israelites would wander in the wilderness for forty years until that generation was dead. On this basis, some have made the interpretation that a generation lasts for forty years. But God used forty years as a measure because the spies had been sent into the Promised Land for forty days, and God counted one year for each day. In Numbers 14, God clearly states this rationale:

> "And the LORD spake unto Moses and unto Aaron, saying, How long *shall I bear with* this evil congregation, which murmur against me? I have heard the murmurings of the children of Israel, which they murmur against me. Say unto them, *As truly as* I live, saith the LORD, as ye have spoken in mine ears, so will I do to you: Your carcases shall fall in this wilderness; and all that were numbered of you, according to your whole number, from twenty years old and upward, which have murmured against me, Doubtless ye shall not come into the land,

concerning which I sware to make you dwell therein, save Caleb the son of Jephunneh, and Joshua the son of Nun. But your little ones, which ye said should be a prey, them will I bring in, and they shall know the land which ye have despised. But *as for* you, your carcases, they shall fall in this wilderness. And your children shall wander in the wilderness forty years, and bear your whoredoms, until your carcases be wasted in the wilderness. After the number of the days in which ye searched the land, *even* forty days, each day for a year, shall ye bear your iniquities, *even* forty years, and ye shall know my breach of promise." (Num. 14:26–34)

Elsewhere, Scripture states both the starting of a generation and the length of it. The length of a person's life is between seventy and eighty years. Psalm 90 says:

"The days of our years *are* threescore years and ten; and if by reason of strength *they be* fourscore years yet *is* their strength labor and sorrow; for it is soon cut off, and we fly away" (Ps. 90:10).

According to data from the World Health Organization, in 2015, human life expectancy worldwide was seventy-one years. In Israel, the life expectancy for males was eighty years. This fits perfectly in the prophecy in the psalm. Since we now know the length of a generation in Scripture, we can ask, "When does a generation start?" In Numbers, God tells Moses to number the tribes from the age of twenty years upward.

"And the LORD spake unto Moses in the wilderness of Sinai, in the tabernacle of the congregation, on the first *day* of the second month, in the second year after they were come out of the land of Egypt, saying, Take ye the sum of all the congregation of the children of Israel, after their families, by the house of their fathers, with the number of *their* names, every male by their polls; From twenty years old and upward, all that are able to go forth to war in Israel: thou and Aaron shall number them by their armies. (Num. 1:1–3)

And they assembled all the congregation together on the first *day* of the second month, and they declared their pedigrees after their families, by the house of their fathers, according to the number of the names, from twenty years old and upward, by their polls. (Num. 1:18)

And the children of Reuben, Israel's eldest son, by their generations, after their families, by the house of their fathers, according to the number of the names, by their polls, every male from twenty years old and upward, all that were able to go forth to war; (Num. 1:20)

Of the children of Simeon, by their generations, after their families, by the house of their fathers, those that were numbered of them, according to the number of the names, by their polls, every male from twenty years old and upward, all that were able to go forth to war; (Num. 1:22)

Of the children of Gad, by their generations, after their families, by the house of their fathers, according to the number of the names, from twenty years old and upward, all that were able to go forth to war; (Num. 1:24)

Of the children of Judah, by their generations, after their families, by the house of their fathers, according to the number of the names, from twenty years old and upward, all that were able to go forth to war; (Num. 1:26)

Of the children of Issachar, by their generations, after their families, by the house of their fathers, according to the number of the names, from twenty years old and upward, all that were able to go forth to war; (Num. 1:28)

Of the children of Zebulun, by their generations, after their families, by the house of their fathers, according to the number of the names, from twenty years old and upward, all that were able to go forth to war; (Num. 1:30)

Of the children of Joseph, *namely*, of the children of Ephraim, by their generations, after their families, by the house of their fathers, according to the number of the names, from twenty years old and upward, all that were able to go forth to war.;(Num. 1:32)

Of the children of Manasseh, by their generations, after their families, by the house of their fathers, according to the number of the names, from twenty years old and upward, all that were able to go forth to war.;(Num. 1:34)

Of the children of Benjamin, by their generations, after their families, by the house of their fathers, according to the number of the names, from twenty years old and upward, all that were able to go forth to war; (Num. 1:36)

Of the children of Dan, by their generations, after their families, by the house of their fathers, according to the number of the names, from twenty years old and upward, all that were able to go forth to war; (Num. 1:38)

Of the children of Asher, by their generations, after their families, by the house of their fathers, according to the number of the names, from twenty years old and upward, all that were able to go forth to war; (Num. 1:40)

Of the children of Naphtali, throughout their generations, after their families, by the house of their fathers, according to the number of the names, from twenty years old and upward, all that were able to go forth to war; (Num. 1:42)

> So were all those that were numbered of the children of
> Israel, by the house of their fathers, from twenty years
> old and upward, all that were able to go forth to war in
> Israel;" (Num. 1:45)

A generation starts at the age of twenty and goes through a human life expectancy of eighty years, giving us a generation length of sixty years. In addition, God declares that for a generation, only males are counted.

According to Daniel, the prophecy given to him was for the Jewish people *and* the Holy City (Jerusalem). Prior to 1948, the Jewish people were scattered throughout the world. In 1948, the nation of Israel reformed, but Jerusalem was not part of the land that Israel controlled at that time, so the seventieth week could *not* begin because the city was not included.

DANIEL'S FIRST SIXTY-NINE WEEKS

In looking at the actual Scripture, remember what Peter says in 2 Peter 1:20:

> "Knowing this first, that no prophecy of the scripture is of any private interpretation." (2 Peter 1:20)

God uses the precise words for what HE is saying. In this book I do not use any private interpretation. I take Scripture exactly as it is written. I DO reference the meaning of a word that is used in the original language when it will make the meaning clear. This is not a private interpretation as it can be easily found by looking up the definition of the word.

In 539 BC, which was the Jewish year 3221, the angel Gabriel came to Daniel and gave him the prophecy of seventy weeks to be given to the Jewish people. Gabriel told Daniel that from the decree to rebuild Jerusalem to the coming of the Messiah, sixty-nine weeks would pass. The word "week" used in Scripture is the Hebrew word "sheb-oo-a" (that is my phonetic spelling) which means a seven-year period. After sixty-nine weeks of seven years per week, the Messiah would be cut off until the time of the seventieth week when He will start His millennial reign.

> "Seventy weeks are determined upon thy people and upon thy holy city, to finish the transgression, and to make an end of sins, and to make reconciliation for iniquity, and to bring in everlasting righteousness, and to seal up the vision and prophecy, and to anoint the most Holy. (Dan 9:24)

> Know therefore and understand, *that* from the going forth
> of the commandment to restore and to build Jerusalem
> unto the Messiah the Prince *shall be* seven weeks, and
> threescore and two weeks: the street shall be built again,
> and the wall, even in troublous times. (Dan 9: 25)

> And after threescore and two weeks shall Messiah be cut
> off, but not for himself: and the people of the prince that
> shall come shall destroy the city and the sanctuary; and
> the end thereof shall be with a flood, and unto the end of
> the war desolations are determined.' (Dan 9:26)

The first sixty-nine weeks started on April 11, 444 BC, which was the tenth of Nisan, Jewish Year 3317. They ended on April 21, AD 31, which was the tenth of Nisan, Jewish year 3791. It was on this day that the prophecy of Exodus 12 was fulfilled:

> "This month *shall be* unto you the beginning of months:
> it *shall be* the first month of the year to you. Speak ye unto
> all the congregation of Israel, saying, In the tenth *day* of
> this month they shall take to them every man a lamb,
> according to the house of *their* fathers, a lamb for an house:
> And if the household be too little for the lamb, let him and
> his neighbor next unto his house take *it* according to the
> number of the souls; every man according to his eating
> shall make your count for the lamb. Your lamb shall be
> without blemish, a male of the first year: ye shall take *it*
> out from the sheep, or from the goats: And ye shall keep
> it up until the fourteenth day of the same month: and the
> whole assembly of the congregation of Israel shall kill it
> in the evening." (Exod. 12:2–6)

Verse 3 states that the Jews were to set aside a lamb on the tenth day of Nisan, in preparation for the sacrifice of the Passover. According to John, Christ and His disciples arrived at the home of Mary, Martha, and Lazarus six days before the Passover:

"Then Jesus six days before the Passover came to Bethany, where Lazarus was which had been dead, whom he raised from the dead. There they made him a supper; and Martha served: but Lazarus was one of them that sat at the table with him" (John 12:1–2).

The moon phase image below shows what the moon in the month of Nisan in AD 31 would have looked like. This is followed by a calendar page showing Scripture passages for events that occurred in that month. Christ and His disciples arrived on a Friday (April 20, AD 31) before the Sabbath, the tenth of Nisan. On the morning of the tenth of Nisan, Christ rode the colt to the temple, turned over the tables and cast out the money changers, and proclaimed that the temple belonged to Him. Passover was on a Wednesday that year, not on a Friday.

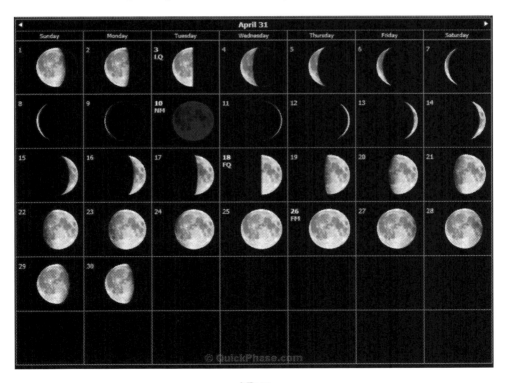

AD 31

April 11, AD 31, showed the thin crescent moon. This day was the twenty-ninth day of Adar, which ended at sunset (6:05 p.m.) and started the month of Nisan. April 12 was therefore the first of Nisan.

April 21, AD 31, was the tenth of Nisan, a Saturday, the day that the Jews were required to separate the Passover lamb and the day that Christ rode into the temple.

April 24 was the fourteenth of Nisan. Passover started at sunset (6:14 p.m.) on that date and ended at sunset (6:14 p.m.) on April 25.

Proof of the Fulfillment of the First Sixty-Nine Weeks

- 69 weeks × 7 years per week = 483 biblical years
- 483 biblical years × 12 months per year = 5,796 months
- 483 biblical years have 67 leap months
- 5,796 regular months + 67 leap months = 5,863 total months
- 1 month = 29 days + 12 hours + 44 minutes + 2.8 seconds = 29.53059 Julian days per month
- 5,863 months × 29.53059 days per month = 173137.84917 Julian days
- Julian day for April 11, 444 BC = JD 1559353
- JD 1559353 + 173137.84917 days = JD 1732490.84917.
- JD 1732490.84917 = Saturday, April 21, AD 31, approximately 10:00 a.m.

Resurrection: Proof of AD 31 Crucifixion

Sunset on April 25, AD 31 (Nisan 14, 3791) was at 6:14 p.m. (JD 1732495.252778), the beginning of the Feast of Unleavened Bread.

Sunrise on April 29, AD 31 (Nisan 18, 3791) was at 4:56 a.m. (JD 1732498.663889) on the Feast of Firstfruits.

From 6:14 p.m. on the Nisan 14 (April 25, AD 31) until 4:56 a.m. on Nisan 18 (April 29, AD 31) = 3 days of 24 hours each + 10 hours

April AD 31 – Jewish Year 3791						
Sunday	Monday	Tuesday	Wednesday	Thursday	Friday	Saturday
1 Adar 19	2 Adar 20	3 Adar 21	4 Adar 22	5 Adar 23	6 Adar 24	7 Adar 25
8 Adar 26	9 Adar 27	10 Adar 28	11 Adar 29	12 Nisan 1	13 Nisan 2	14 Nisan 3
15 Nisan 4	16 Nisan 5	17 Nisan 6	18 Nisan 7	19 Nisan 8	20 Nisan 9 Christ arrives in Bethany in time for supper	21 Nisan 10 Christ rides to temple and claims it as His
22 Nisan 11	23 Nisan 12	24 Nisan 13 Nisan 14 starts at sunset	25 Nisan 14 Passover	26 Nisan 15 Feast of Unleavened Bread	27 Nisan 16	28 Nisan 17
29 Nisan 18 Feast of Firstfruits	30 Nisan 19					

This leaves only the seventieth week of Daniel's prophecy left to be fulfilled. According to Daniel 9, the Antichrist will desecrate the altar in the temple that has been rebuilt and will proclaim himself as God.

> "And from the time that the daily sacrifice shall be taken away, and the abomination that makes desolate set up, there shall be a thousand two hundred and ninety days." (Dan. 12:11).

As we approach the end of this last generation, we look at the timing for when a treaty or an agreement might be signed with Israel. Israel signs its treaties on Rosh Hashanah, which in Jewish tradition is the anniversary of the creation of the world. The midpoint of a seven-year treaty would be 1,260 days from the signing. According to God, from the desecration of the altar until the end, another 1,290 days will pass, for a total of 2,550 days from the signing of the agreement until eternity starts.

It is the final week that this book deals with. The calendars I have included are for seven years and goes from Rosh Hashanah on day one until Yom Kippur seven years later, for precisely 2,550 days.

During this time, there will be events that are called the great tribulation, or the time of Jacob's trouble. It will be a terrible time and there has never been tribulation like it since the creation of humankind. (Matt. 24:21)

In Dan 6:24, we are told that a total of seventy weeks has been given to the Jews and the city of Jerusalem. In verse 25, we are told that the seventy weeks will start with the decree to rebuild Jerusalem. Scripture also tells us that the seventy weeks will be divided into two parts. The first sixty-nine weeks began when the decree to rebuild Jerusalem began in 444 BC (3317 in the Jewish calendar) when Artaxerxes issued the decree to Nehemiah, and ended on Saturday, April 21, AD 31. This was exactly sixty-nine weeks, calculated as seven years per week, or precisely 173,137 days.

In AD 70, the Roman army destroyed the city of Jerusalem, including the temple. The Jewish people were then scattered over the world until

May 14, 1948 when Israel declared itself a nation. Verse 26 tells us that the prince that shall come must be a Roman (from Rome). Verse 27 tells us that this prince (leader) that shall come will sign an agreement that will be for "one week." God also tells us that in the middle of the duration of the agreement, it will be broken. The altar will be desecrated, and an idol will be set up.

This started the last generation before eternity. We are currently living in that last generation. This is the time which Jesus Christ said this generation will not pass until everything He spoke of has come to pass. This calendar does *not* determine when the rapture of the believers will occur. However, as we approach the end of the generation, I pray that, if you have not repented and turned your life to Christ, you will do so. There is only one resurrection of the righteous dead and only one catching away of the living righteous. If this occurs, before you turn your life to Jesus Christ, then your eternity will have been decided by your own choice.

> "When once the master of the house is risen up, and hath shut to the door, and ye begin to stand without, and to knock at the door, saying, Lord, Lord, open unto us; and he shall answer and say unto you, I know you not whence ye are: Then shall ye begin to say, We have eaten and drunk in thy presence, and thou hast taught in our streets. But he shall say, I tell you, I know you not whence ye are; depart from me, all *ye* workers of iniquity. There shall be weeping and gnashing of teeth, when ye shall see Abraham, and Isaac, and Jacob, and all the prophets, in the kingdom of God, and you *yourselves* thrust out." (Luke 13: 25-28)

> "Then shall the kingdom of heaven be likened unto ten virgins, which took their lamps, and went forth to meet the bridegroom. And five of them were wise, and five *were* foolish. They that *were* foolish took their lamps, and took no oil with them: But the wise took oil in their

vessels with their lamps. While the bridegroom tarried, they all slumbered and slept. And at midnight there was a cry made, Behold, the bridegroom cometh; go ye out to meet him. Then all those virgins arose, and trimmed their lamps. And the foolish said unto the wise, Give us of your oil; for our lamps are gone out. But the wise answered, saying, *Not so*; lest there be not enough for us and you: but go ye rather to them that sell, and buy for yourselves. And while they went to buy, the bridegroom came; and they that were ready went in with him to the marriage: and the door was shut. Afterward came also the other virgins, saying, Lord, Lord, open to us. But he answered and said, Verily I say unto you, I know you not." (Mat 25:1-12)

The calendar in this book shows events that will occur before the end time. If believers in Christ are caught away to heaven before you repent, you will have to face a period of tribulation unlike anything seen since the creation of the world. According to Scripture, once the last seven years starts, the population of the earth will be reduced from approximately 7.5 billion people to fewer than 3.5 billion people. This reduction will occur worldwide. It will not happen because of the acts of any one country, but because of the world's rebellion against God. In case you think that you will be unaffected by this, consider what it would be like if the country you live in were to lose half of its population within one year.

DANIEL'S SEVENTIETH WEEK

On June 7, 1967, the Israeli military reclaimed Jerusalem and the Temple Mount. This event placed the Holy City under the control of the Jewish people. The seventieth week could now be fulfilled.

> "Seventy weeks are determined upon thy people and upon thy holy city, to finish the transgression, and to make an end of sins, and to make reconciliation for iniquity, and to bring in everlasting righteousness, and to seal up the vision and prophecy, and to anoint the most Holy." (Dan. 9:24)

The disciples asked Christ what the signs would be of His coming. Christ gave the signs along with the parable of the fig tree. He ended with these statements:

> "So likewise ye, when ye shall see all these things, know that it is near, *even* at the doors. Verily I say unto you, this generation shall not pass, till all these things be fulfilled." (Matt. 24:33–34)

> "So ye in like manner, when ye shall see these things come to pass, know that it is nigh, *even* at the doors. Verily I say unto you, that this generation shall not pass, till all these things be done." (Mark 13:29–30)

> "So likewise ye, when ye see these things come to pass, know ye that the kingdom of God is nigh at hand. Verily

> I say unto you, this generation shall not pass away, till all
> be fulfilled." (Luke 21:31–32)

We have just finished the fiftieth year since the liberation of Jerusalem and the Temple Mount. The generation that started on June 7, 1967, was the first generation that saw the Jewish people with control over the Holy City in 1,897 years. This means there are only ten years remaining in the last generation before eternity starts. Of the remaining ten years, there is only one seven-year week that has the proper number of days in it so that *all* the prophecies will accurately fit.

The last year of the seven-year window will be the Jewish year 5787. It will end on Yom Kippur, which is the sixtieth year of the generation. This is the generation that Jesus said would not pass until everything that is prophesied has come to pass.

Many preachers and laymen claim that in Revelation 4, when John is told to "come up here," this represents the "rapture" of the church. This error is pushed by many. This allows them to take all the seals, trumpets, and vials of the wrath of God and lump them together as God's wrath or God's judgments.

> ".....Come up hither, and I will shew thee things which
> must be hereafter." (Rev 4: 1).

The word translated as "up" is the Greek word *anabaino*, which simply means "to ascend." This is the same word used when Christ went "up" to the Mount of Olives. Compare this to the word used in 1 Thessalonians:

> "Then we which are alive *and* remain shall be caught up
> together with them in the clouds, to meet the Lord in the
> air: and so shall we ever be with the Lord." (1 Thess. 4:17).

This is the Greek word *harpazo*, which means to "snatch out or away." You can see that when God means simply to "come up," He knows which word to use. When He means that He is going to "snatch us away," He also knows the precise word for that precise meaning.

"And after threescore and two weeks shall Messiah be cut
off, but not for himself: and the people of the prince that
shall come shall destroy the city and the sanctuary; and
the end thereof *shall* be with a flood, and unto the end of
the war desolations are determined. And he shall confirm
the covenant with many for one week: and in the midst
of the week he shall cause the sacrifice and the oblation
to cease, and for the overspreading of abominations he
shall make *it* desolate, even until the consummation,
and that determined shall be poured upon the desolate."
(Dan 9:26-27)

Verse 26 tells us that the people of the prince (leader) that is to come shall
destroy the city and the sanctuary. In AD 70, the Roman army destroyed
the city of Jerusalem, including the temple. The Jewish people were then
scattered over the world until May 14, 1948 when Israel declared itself a
nation. Verse 26 tells us that the prince that shall come must be a Roman
(from Rome). Verse 27 tells us that this prince (leader) that shall come will
sign an agreement that will be for "one week." God also tells us that in
the middle of the duration of the agreement, it will be broken. The altar
will be desecrated, and an idol will be set up.

From AD 70 until AD 1967, Jews were not in control of the city of
Jerusalem. On June 7, 1967, Jews regained control of Jerusalem. As of
that day, all the requirements for the final week were in place for the first
time since Christ's first coming. This started the last generation before
eternity.

We are currently living in the last generation. This is the time about
which Jesus Christ said that this generation will not pass until everything
He spoke of has come to pass. The calendar lasts seven years and goes
from Rosh Hashanah on day one until Yom Kippur seven years later, or
precisely 2,550 days.

This calendar does *not* determine when the rapture of the believers will
occur. However, as we approach the end of the generation, I pray that, if

you have not repented and turned your life to Christ, you will do so. There is only one resurrection of the righteous dead and only one catching away of the living righteous. If this occurs before you turn your life to Jesus Christ, then your eternity will have been decided by your own choice.

Approximately two thousand five hundred years ago, God proclaimed that there would be a set period of time from the going forth of the decree to restore and to build Jerusalem until He ends the world (Dan. 9:24–25). He told Daniel the prophet, in captivity in Babylon, that seventy weeks had been determined for the Jewish people to bring about the Messiah, the church age, and His final return to take the world and set up His reign as King of Kings and Lord of Lords.

This book is different from previous works you may have read. This book relies heavily on the movement of the moon to determine days, months, and years for prophecies.

> "He appointed the moon for seasons: the sun knoweth his going down" (Ps. 104:19).

In this verse, God is stating that He has chosen the moon to show His appointed times. The word translated as "seasons" is the Hebrew word *moed*, which refers to God's appointed times. This word has nothing to do with seasons as we define them in Western cultures (winter, spring, summer, and fall). The same word used in Leviticus 23, where God proclaims His feast days.

God is very precise in His wording. He uses words appropriately and in context with what He wants Scripture to say. In Scripture, God proclaimed that a month is measured from the first crescent of the new moon to the following crescent of the new moon. Nowhere in Scripture does God change the method for determining a month.

The beginning of the new month is when the first crescent of the moon can be seen after the moon has gone dark.

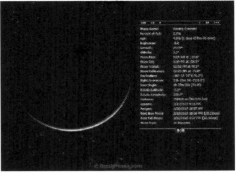

(New moon—Dark of the moon)

Dark of moon at sunset
in Jerusalem, Israel

(Crescent moon)

Crescent of new moon at sunset
in Jerusalem, Israel

These images show what the moon looks like at the end of one month and the beginning of the next month. Sightings of the crescent of the new moon can only occur at sunset and can only be seen for between fifteen and ninety minutes. Then the moon sets.

There are three basic ways a book like this can be written. The first and easiest is to simply make a claim without any proof. This leaves it up to the reader to determine if the author is right. The second way, which is harder, is to provide a calendar that gives a visual of what the author is saying. Again, it is up to the reader to determine if the author has given proof that the calendar is accurate. The third way is to provide not only a calendar, but proof of the moon phases and the starting and ending dates of the given month. This is the option that I have taken. For each calendar page provided, I also provide a page showing the applicable moon phases for that month. The purpose is to provide you with proof of the accuracy that God has given us.

The calendar pages I have depicted deal *only* with God's appointed times. They do not include the Jewish festivals and holidays that God has not declared His appointed times, as listed in Leviticus 23.

Calendar Including Seals, Trumpets, and Bowls of Wrath

September 2019 (Jewish Year 5779/5780)						
Sunday	Monday	Tuesday	Wednesday	Thursday	Friday	Saturday
1 Elul 1	2 Elul 2	3 Elul 3	4 Elul 4	5 Elul 5	6 Elul 6	7 Elul 7
8 Elul 8	9 Elul 9	10 Elul 10	11 Elul 11	12 Elul 12	13 Elul 13	14 Elul 14
15 Elul 15	16 Elul 16	17 Elul 17	18 Elul 18	19 Elul 19	20 Elul 20	21 Elul 21
22 Elul 22	23 Elul 23	24 Elul 24	25 Elul 25	26 Elul 26	27 Elul 27	28 Elul 28
29 Elul 29	30 Tishri 1 JD2458756 1	*September 29*: Elul 29 ends at sunset (5:29 p.m.) and becomes Tishri 1. Tishri is the seventh month of the Jewish year and has thirty days.				

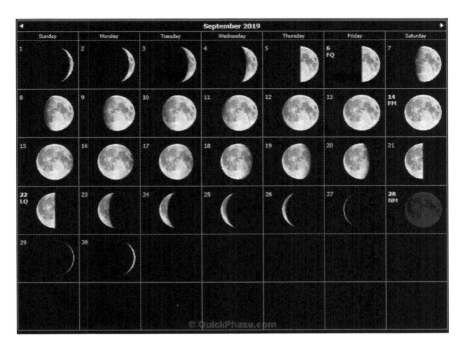

September 2019

Titles for Tishri 1

Rosh Hashanah

Feast of Trumpets

The Awakening Blast of the Righteous

The Coronation of the Messiah

The Marriage Supper of the Messiah

The Judgment of the Righteous

The Opening of the Books of Judgment

The Day that No Man Knows (Matthew 24:36; Mark 13:32)

October 2019 (Jewish Year 5780)						
Sunday	Monday	Tuesday	Wednesday	Thursday	Friday	Saturday
		1 Tishri 2 2	2 Tishri 3 3	3 Tishri 4 4	4 Tishri 5 5	5 Tishri 6 6
6 Tishri 7 7	7 Tishri 8 8	8 Tishri 9 9	9 Tishri 10 10	10 Tishri 11 11	11 Tishri 12 12	12 Tishri 13 13
13 Tishri 14 14	14 Tishri 15 15	15 Tishri 16 16	16 Tishri 17 17	17 Tishri 18 18	18 Tishri 19 19	19 Tishri 20 20
20 Tishri 21 21	21 Tishri 22 22	22 Tishri 23 23	23 Tishri 24 24	24 Tishri 25 25	25 Tishri 26 26	26 Tishri 27 27
27 Tishri 28 28	28 Tishri 29 29	29 Tishri 30 30	30 Cheshvan 1 31	31 Cheshvan 2 32		

Rosh Chodesh Cheshvan

October 29: Tishri 30 ends at sunset (4:54 p.m.) and starts Cheshvan 1. Cheshvan is the eighth month of the Jewish year and has either twenty-nine or thirty days, depending on the new moon.

Cheshvan 1: Possible opening of first seal.

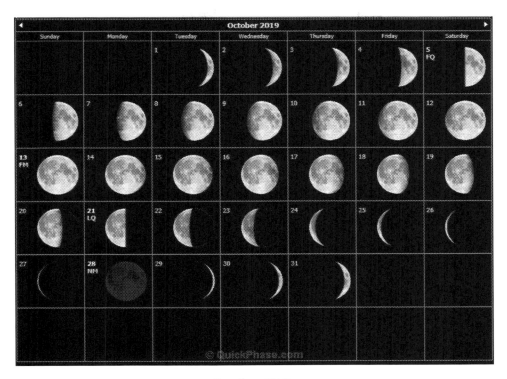

October 2019>

November 2019 (Jewish Year 5780)						
Sunday	Monday	Tuesday	Wednesday	Thursday	Friday	Saturday
					1 Cheshvan 3 **33**	**2** Cheshvan 4 **34**
3 Cheshvan 5 **35**	**4** Cheshvan 6 **36**	**5** Cheshvan 7 **37**	**6** Cheshvan 8 **38**	**7** Cheshvan 9 **39**	**8** Cheshvan 10 **40**	**9** Cheshvan 11 **41**
10 Cheshvan 12 **42**	**11** Cheshvan 13 **43**	**12** Cheshvan 14 **44**	**13** Cheshvan 15 **45**	**14** Cheshvan 16 **46**	**15** Cheshvan 17 **47**	**16** Cheshvan 18 **48**
17 Cheshvan 19 **49**	**18** Cheshvan 20 **50**	**19** Cheshvan 21 **51**	**20** Cheshvan 22 **52**	**21** Cheshvan 23 **53**	**22** Cheshvan 24 **54**	**23** Cheshvan 25 **55**
24 Cheshvan 26 **56**	**25** Cheshvan 27 **57**	**26** Cheshvan 28 **58**	**27** Cheshvan 29 **59**	**28** Cheshvan 30 **60**	**29** Kislev 1 **61**	**30** Kislev 2 **62**

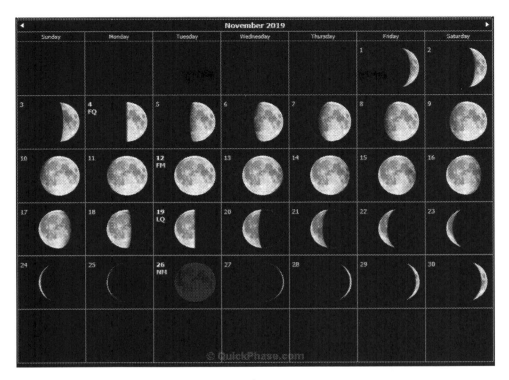

November 2019

Rosh Chodesh Kislev

November 28: Cheshvan 30 ends at sunset (4:35 p.m.) and starts Kislev 1.

November 29: Kislev 1 ends at sunset. Kislev is the ninth month of the Jewish calendar and has either twenty-nine or thirty days, depending on the new moon.

December 2019 (Jewish Year 5780)						
Sunday	**Monday**	**Tuesday**	**Wednesday**	**Thursday**	**Friday**	**Saturday**
1 Kislev 3 63	2 Kislev 4 64	3 Kislev 5 65	4 Kislev 6 66	5 Kislev 7 67	6 Kislev 8 68	7 Kislev 9 69
8 Kislev 10 70	9 Kislev 11 71	10 Kislev 12 72	11 Kislev 13 73	12 Kislev 14 74	13 Kislev 15 75	14 Kislev 16 76
15 Kislev 17 77	16 Kislev 18 78	17 Kislev 19 79	18 Kislev 20 80	19 Kislev 21 81	20 Kislev 22 82	21 Kislev 23 83
22 Kislev 24 84	23 Kislev 25 85	24 Kislev 26 86	25 Kislev 27 87	26 Kislev 28 88	27 Kislev 29 89	28 Kislev 30 90
29 Tevet 1 91	30 Tevet 2 92	31 Tevet 3 93	Kislev 30 ends at sunset (4:43 p.m.) and starts Tevet 1.		

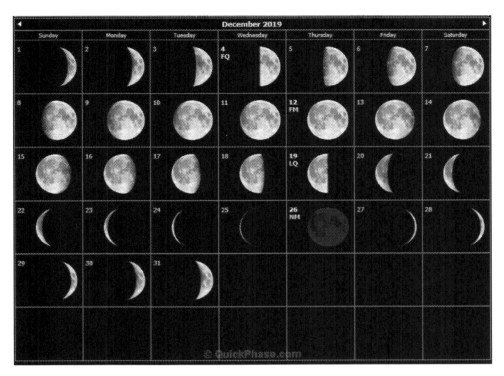

December 2019

December 28: Kislev 30 ends at sunset (4:43 p.m.) and starts Tevet 1. Tevet is the tenth month of the Jewish calendar and has twenty-nine days.

January 2020 (Jewish Year 5780)						
Sunday	Monday	Tuesday	Wednesday	Thursday	Friday	Saturday
Tevet is the tenth month of the Jewish calendar and has twenty-nine days.			**1** Tevet 4 94	**2** Tevet 5 95	**3** Tevet 6 96	**4** Tevet 7 97
5 Tevet 8 98	**6** Tevet 9 99	**7** Tevet 10 100	**8** Tevet 11 101	**9** Tevet 12 102	**10** Tevet 13 103	**11** Tevet 14 104
12 Tevet 15 105	**13** Tevet 16 106	**14** Tevet 17 107	**15** Tevet 18 108	**16** Tevet 19 109	**17** Tevet 20 110	**18** Tevet 21 111
19 Tevet 22 112	**20** Tevet 23 113	**21** Tevet 24 114	**22** Tevet 25 115	**23** Tevet 26 116	**24** Tevet 27 117	**25** Tevet 28 118
26 Tevet 2 9 119	**27** Sh'vat 1 120	**28** Sh'vat 2 121	**29** Sh'vat 3 122	**30** Sh'vat 4 123	**31** Sh'vat 5 124	

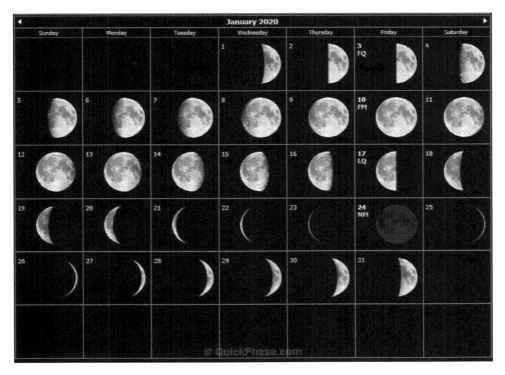

January 2020

January 27: Sh'vat 1 ends at sunset. Sh'vat is the eleventh month of the Jewish calendar and has thirty days.

Sh'vat 1: Possible opening of second seal.

February 2020 (Jewish Year 5780)						
Sunday	Monday	Tuesday	Wednesday	Thursday	Friday	Saturday
Sh'vat is the eleventh month of the Jewish calendar and has thirty days. Adar 1: Possible opening of third seal.						**1** Sh'vat 6 125
2 Sh'vat 7 126	**3** Sh'vat 8 127	**4** Sh'vat 9 128	**5** Sh'vat 10 129	**6** Sh'vat 11 130	**7** Sh'vat 12 131	**8** Sh'vat 13 132
9 Sh'vat 14 133	**10** Sh'vat 15 134	**11** Sh'vat 16 135	**12** Sh'vat 17 136	**13** Sh'vat 18 137	**14** Sh'vat 19 138	**15** Sh'vat 20 139
16 Sh'vat 21 140	**17** Sh'vat 22 141	**18** Sh'vat 23 142	**19** Sh'vat 24 143	**20** Sh'vat 25 144	**21** Sh'vat 26 145	**22** Sh'vat 27 146
23 Sh'vat 28 147	**24** Sh'vat 29 148	**25** Sh'vat 30 149	**26** Adar 1 150	**27** Adar 2 151	**28** Adar 3 152	**29** Adar 4 153

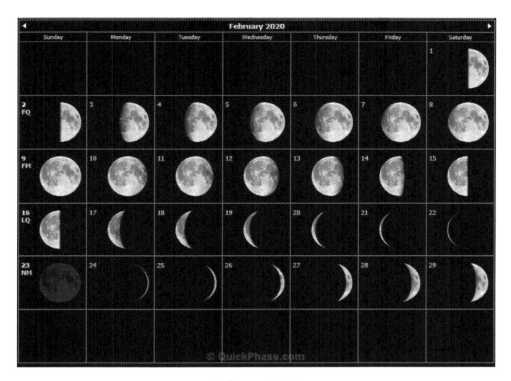

February 2020

February 25: Sh'vat 30 ends at sunset (5:35 p.m.) and starts Adar 1.

March 2020 (Jewish Year 5780)						
Sunday	Monday	Tuesday	Wednesday	Thursday	Friday	Saturday
1 Adar 5 154	2 Adar 6 155	3 Adar 7 156	4 Adar 8 157	5 Adar 9 158	6 Adar 10 159	7 Adar 11 160
8 Adar 12 161	9 Adar 13 162	10 Adar 14 163	11 Adar 15 164	12 Adar 16 165	13 Adar 17 166	14 Adar 18 167
15 Adar 19 168	16 Adar 20 169	17 Adar 21 170	18 Adar 22 171	19 Adar 23 172	20 Adar24 173	21 Adar 25 174
22 Adar 26 175	23 Adar 27 176	24 Adar 28 177	25 Adar 29 178	26 Nisan 1 179	27 Nisan 2 180	28 Nisan 3 181
29 Nisan 4 182	30 Nisan 5 183	31 Nisan 6 184	Adar is the twelfth month of the Jewish year and has 29 days. *March 25*: Adar 29 ends at sunset (5:57 p.m.) and starts the month of Nisan.			

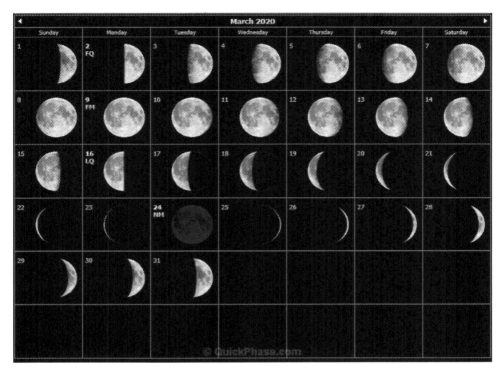

March 2020

Rosh Chodesh Nisan

March 25: Adar 29 ends at sunset (5:57 p.m.) and starts the month of Nisan.

March 26: Nisan 1 ends at sunset. Nisan is the first month of the Jewish year and has thirty days.

Nisan 1: Opening of the fourth seal: "And I looked and behold a pale horse: and his name that sat on him was Death, and Hell followed with him. And power was given unto them over the fourth part of the earth, to kill with sword, and with hunger, and with death, and with the beasts of the earth. Possible date for the arrival of the two witnesses" (Rev. 6:7–8).

April 2020 (Jewish Year 5780)						
Sunday	Monday	Tuesday	Wednesday	Thursday	Friday	Saturday
Lyyar is the second month of the Jewish year and has twenty-nine days			1 Nisan 7 185	2 Nisan 8 186	3 Nisan 9 187	4 Nisan 10 188
5 Nisan 11 189	6 Nisan 12 190	7 Nisan 13 191	8 Nisan 14 192	9 Nisan 15 193	10 Nisan 16 194	11 Nisan 17 195
12 Nisan 18 196	13 Nisan 19 197	14 Nisan 20 198	15 Nisan 21 199	16 Nisan 22 200	16 Nisan 23 201	18 Nisan 24 202
19 Nisan 25 203	20 Nisan 26 204	21 Nisan 27 205	22 Nisan 28 206	23 Nisan 29 207	24 Nisan 30 208	25 Lyyar 1 209
26 Lyyar 2 210	27 Lyyar 3 211	28 Lyyar 4 212	29 Lyyar 5 213	30 Lyyar 6 214		

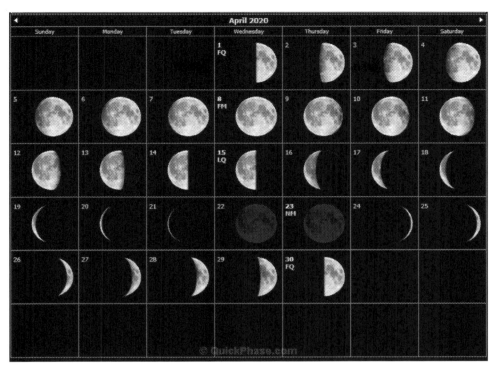

April 2020

May 2020 (Jewish Year 5780)						
Sunday	Monday	Tuesday	Wednesday	Thursday	Friday	Saturday
May 22 or *Lyyar 28*: Yom Yerushalayim, the fifty-third anniversary of Israel reclaiming the Holy City (Jerusalem).					**1** Lyyar 7 215	**2** Lyyar 8 216
3 Lyyar 9 217	**4** Lyyar 10 218	**5** Lyyar 11 219	**6** Lyyar 12 220	**7** Lyyar 13 221	**8** Lyyar 14 222	**9** Lyyar 15 223
10 Lyyar 16 224	**11** Lyyar 17 225	**12** Lyyar 18 226	**13** Lyyar 19 227	**14** Lyyar 20 228	**15** Lyyar 21 229	**16** Lyyar 22 230
17 Lyyar 23 231	**18** Lyyar 24 232	**19** Lyyar 25 233	**20** Lyyar 26 234	**21** Lyyar 27 235	**22** Lyyar 28 236	**23** Lyyar 29 237
24 Sivan 1 238	**25** Sivan 2 239	**26** Sivan 3 240	**27** Sivan 4 241	**28** Sivan 5 242	**29** Sivan 6 243	**30** Sivan 7 244
31 Sivan 8 245	*May 23*: Lyyar 29 ends at sunset (6:40 p.m.) and begins the month of Sivan. Sivan is the third month of the Jewish year and has thirty days.					

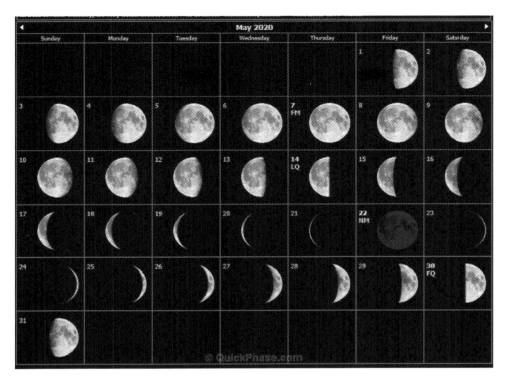

May 2020

Rosh Chodesh Sivan

May 23: Lyyar 29 ends at sunset (6:40 p.m.) and begins the month of Sivan.

June 2020 (Jewish Year 5780)						
Sunday	Monday	Tuesday	Wednesday	Thursday	Friday	Saturday
	1 Sivan 9 246	**2** Sivan 10 247	**3** Sivan 11 248	**4** Sivan 12 249	**5** Sivan 13 250	**6** Sivan 14 251
7 Sivan 15 252	**8** Sivan 16 253	**9** Sivan 17 254	**10** Sivan 18 255	**11** Sivan 19 256	**12** Sivan 20 257	**13** Sivan 21 258
14 Sivan 22 259	**15** Sivan 23 260	**16** Sivan 24 261	**17** Sivan 25 262	**18** Sivan 26 263	**19** Sivan 27 264	**20** Sivan 28 265
21 Sivan 29 266	**22** Sivan 30 267	**23** Tamuz 1 268	**24** Tamuz 2 269	**25** Tamuz 3 270	**26** Tamuz 4 271	**27** Tamuz 5 272
28 Tamuz 6 273	**29** Tamuz 7 274	**30** Tamuz 8 275	Tamuz is the fourth month of the Jewish year and has twenty-nine days.			

June 22: Sivan 30 ends at sunset (6:54 p.m.) and begins Tamuz 1.

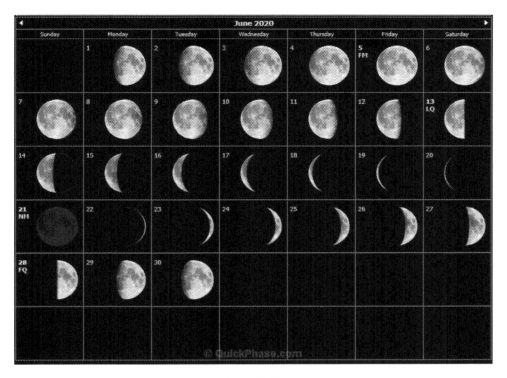

June 2020

July 2020 (Jewish Year 5780)						
Sunday	Monday	Tuesday	Wednesday	Thursday	Friday	Saturday
Tamuz 29: Possible opening of the fifth seal.			1 Tamuz 9 276	2 Tamuz 10 277	3 Tamuz 11 278	4 Tamuz 12 279
5 Tamuz 13 280	6 Tamuz 14 281	7 Tamuz 15 282	8 Tamuz 16 283	9 Tamuz 17 284	10 Tamuz 18 285	11 Tamuz 19 286
12 Tamuz 20 287	13 Tamuz 21 288	14 Tamuz 22 289	15 Tamuz 23 290	16 Tamuz 24 291	17 Tamuz 25 292	18 Tamuz 26 293
19 Tamuz 27 294	20 Tamuz 28 295	21 Tamuz 29 296	22 Av 1 297	23 Av 2 298	24 Av 3 299	25 Av 4 300
26 Av 5 301	27 Av 6 302	28 Av 7 303	29 Av 8 304	30 Av 9 305	31 Av 10 306	

Rosh Chodesh Av

July 21: Tamuz 29 ends at sunset (6:48 p.m.) and begins the month of Av. Av is the fifth month of the Jewish year and has thirty days.

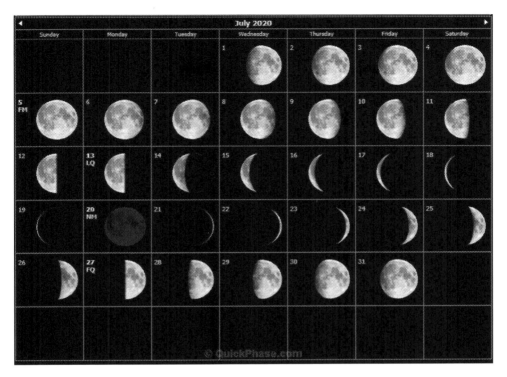

July 2020

Tamuz 29: Opening of the fifth seal: "And when he had opened the fifth seal, I saw under the altar the souls of them that were slain for the word of God, and for the testimony which they held" (Rev. 6:9).

August 2020 (Jewish Year 5780)						
Sunday	Monday	Tuesday	Wednesday	Thursday	Friday	Saturday
August 20: Av 30 ends at sunset (6:21 p.m.) and begins the month of Elul. *August 21*: Elul 1 ends at sunset. Elul is the sixth month of the Jewish year and has twenty-nine days.						**1** Av 11 307
2 Av 12 308	**3** Av 13 309	**4** Av 14 310	**5** Av 15 311	**6** Av 16 312	**7** Av 17 313	**8** Av 18 314
9 Av 19 315	**10** Av 20 316	**11** Av 21 317	**12** Av 22 318	**13** Av 23 319	**14** Av 24 320	**15** Av 25 321
16 Av 26 322	**17** Av 27 323	**18** Av 28 324	**19** Av 29 325	**20** Av 30 326	**21** Elul 1 327	**22** Elul 2 328
23 Elul 3 329	**24** Elul 4 330	**25** Elul 5 331	**26** Elul 6 332	**27** Elul 7 333	**28** Elul 8 334	**29** Elul 9 335
30 Elul 10 336	**31** Elul 11 337	August 20: Rosh Chodesh Elul Elul1: Possible opening of the sixth seal				

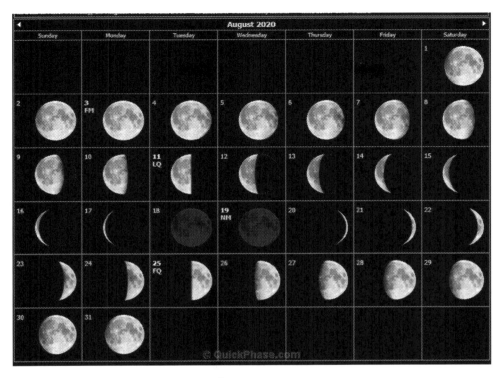

August 2020

September 2020 (Jewish Year 5780-5781)						
Sunday	Monday	Tuesday	Wednesday	Thursday	Friday	Saturday
		1 Elul 12 338	2 Elul 13 339	3 Elul 14 340	4 Elul 15 341	5 Elul 16 342
6 Elul 17 343	7 Elul 18 344	8 Elul 19 345	9 Elul 20 346	10 Elul 21 347	11 Elul 22 348	12 Elul 23 349
13 Elul 24 350	14 Elul 25 351	15 Elul 26 352	16 Elul 27 353	17 Elul 28 354	18 Elul 29 355	19 Tishri 1 356
20 Tishri 2 357	21 Tishri 3 358	22 Tishri 4 359	23 Tishri 5 360	24 Tishri 6 361	25 Tishri 7 362	26 Tishri 8 363
27 Tishri 9 364	28 Tishri 10 365	29 Tishri 11 366	30 Tishri 12 367	September 18: Rosh Chodesh Tishri		

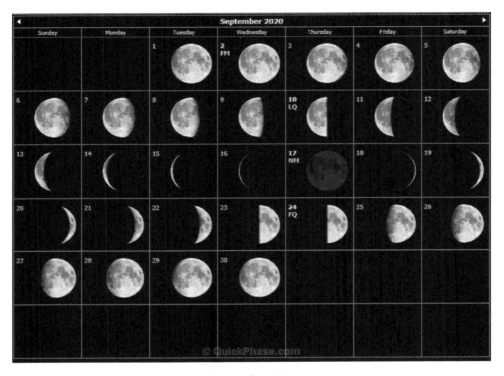

September 2020

October 2020 (Jewish Year 5781)						
Sunday	Monday	Tuesday	Wednesday	Thursday	Friday	Saturday
October 18: Rosh Chodesh Cheshvan *October 19*: Possible opening of the seventh seal.				**1** Tishri 13 368	**2** Tishri 14 369	**3** Tishri 15 370
4 Tishri 16 371	**5** Tishri 17 372	**6** Tishri 18 373	**7** Tishri 19 374	**8** Tishri 20 375	**9** Tishri 21 376	**10** Tishri 22 377
11 Tishri 23 378	**12** Tishri 24 379	**13** Tishri 25 380	**14** Tishri 26 381	**15** Tishri 27 382	**16** Tishri 28 383	**17** Tishri 29 384
18 Tishri 30 385	**19** Cheshvan 1 386	**20** Cheshvan 2 387	**21** Cheshvan 3 388	**22** Cheshvan 4 389	**23** Cheshvan 5 390	**24** Cheshvan 6 391
25 Cheshvan 7 392	**26** Cheshvan 8 393	**27** Cheshvan 9 394	**28** Cheshvan 10 395	**29** Cheshvan 11 396	**30** Cheshvan 12 397	**31** Cheshvan 13 398

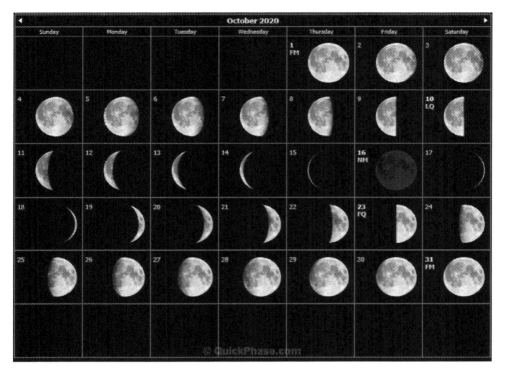

October 2020

Rosh Chodesh Cheshvan

October 18: Tishri 30 ends at sunset (5:04 p.m.) and begins Cheshvan 1.

October 19: Cheshvan 1 lasts until sunset. Cheshvan is the eighth month of the Jewish calendar and has twenty-nine or thirty days, depending on the new moon.

Cheshvan 1: Possible opening of the seventh seal: "And when he had opened the seventh seal, there was silence in heaven about the space of half an hour" (Rev 8:1).

November 2020 (Jewish Year 5781)						
Sunday	Monday	Tuesday	Wednesday	Thursday	Friday	Saturday
1 Cheshvan 14 399	2 Cheshvan 15 400	3 Cheshvan 16 401	4 Cheshvan 17 402	5 Cheshvan 18 403	6 Cheshvan 19 404	7 Cheshvan 20 405
8 Cheshvan 21 406	9 Cheshvan 22 407	10 Cheshvan 23 408	11 Cheshvan 24 409	12 Cheshvan 25 410	13 Cheshvan 26 411	14 Cheshvan 27 412
15 Cheshvan 28 413	16 Cheshvan 29 414	17 Kislev 1 415	18 Kislev 2 416	19 Kislev 3 417	20 Kislev 4 418	21 Kislev 5 419
22 Kislev 6 420	23 Kislev 7 421	24 Kislev 8 422	25 Kislev 9 423	26 Kislev 10 424	27 Kislev 11 425	28 Kislev 12 426
29 Kislev 13 427	30 Kislev 14 428	*November 16:* Rosh Chodesh Kislev *November 17:* Sounding of the first trumpet.				

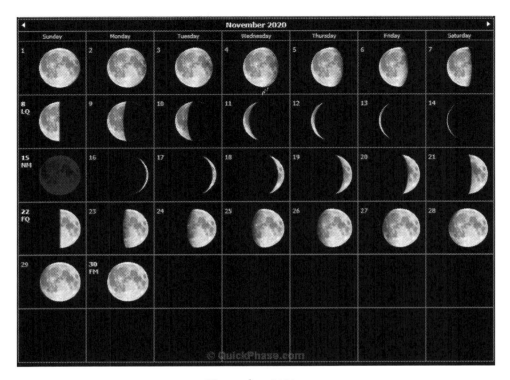

November 2020>

November 16: Cheshvan 29 ends at sunset (4:39 p.m.) and immediately begins Kislev 1.

November 17: Kislev 1 ends at sunset. Kislev is the ninth month of the Jewish calendar and has twenty-nine or thirty days, depending on the new moon.

Kislev 1: Possible sounding of the first trumpet: "The first angel sounded, and there followed hail and fire mingled with blood, and they were cast upon the earth: and the third part of trees was burnt up, and all green grass was burnt up" (Rev. 8:7).

December 2020 (Jewish Year 5781)						
Sunday	Monday	Tuesday	Wednesday	Thursday	Friday	Saturday
December 17: Sounding of the second trumpet.		**1** Kislev 15 *429*	**2** Kislev 16 *430*	**3** Kislev 17 *431*	**4** Kislev 18 *432*	**5** Kislev 19 *433*
6 Kislev 20 *434*	**7** Kislev 21 *435*	**8** Kislev 22 *436*	**9** Kislev 23 *437*	**10** Kislev 24 *438*	**11** Kislev 25 *439*	**12** Kislev 26 *440*
13 Kislev 27 *441*	**14** Kislev 28 *442*	**15** Kislev 29 *443*	**16** Kislev 30 *444*	**17** Tevet 1 *445*	**18** Tevet 2 *446*	**19** Tevet 3 *447*
20 Tevet 4 *448*	**21** Tevet 5 *449*	**22** Tevet 6 *450*	**23** Tevet 7 *451*	**24** Tevet 8 *452*	**25** Tevet 9 *453*	**26** Tevet 10 *454*
27 Tevet 11 *455*	**28** Tevet 12 *456*	**29** Tevet 13 *457*	**30** Tevet 14 *458*	**31** Tevet 15 *459*		

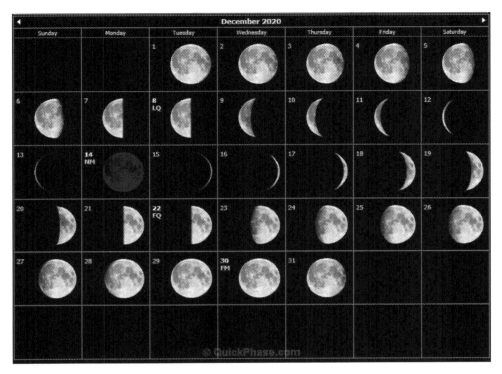

December 2020

December 16: Kislev 30 ends at sunset (4:37 p.m.) and begins Tevet 1.

December 17: Tevet 1 ends at sunset. Tevet is the tenth month of the Jewish calendar and has twenty-nine days.

Tevet 1: Sounding of the second trumpet (Rev. 8:8–9). Possible asteroid impact: one third of the sea becomes blood, one third of the creatures in the sea die, and one third of ships are destroyed.

January 2021 (Jewish Year 5781)						
Sunday	Monday	Tuesday	Wednesday	Thursday	Friday	Saturday
January 15: Sh'vat 1 ends at sunset. Sh'vat is the eleventh month of the Jewish calendar and has thirty days.					**1** Tevet 16 460	**2** Tevet 17 461
3 Tevet 18 462	**4** Tevet 19 463	**5** Tevet 20 464	**6** Tevet 21 465	**7** Tevet 22 466	**8** Tevet 23 467	**9** Tevet 24 468
10 Tevet 25 469	**11** Tevet 26 470	**12** Tevet 27 471	**13** Tevet 28 472	**14** Tevet 29 473	**15** Sh'vat 1 474	**16** Sh'vat 2 475
17 Sh'vat 3 476	**18** Sh'vat 4 477	**19** Sh'vat 5 478	**20** Sh'vat 6 479	**21** Sh'vat 7 480	**22** Sh'vat 8 481	**23** Sh'vat 9 482
24 Sh'vat 10 483	**25** Sh'vat 11 484	**26** Sh'vat 12 485	**27** Sh'vat 13 486	**28** Sh'vat 14 487	**29** Sh'vat 15 488	**30** Sh'vat 16 489
31 Sh'vat 17 490	*January 15*: Sounding of the third trumpet (Rev. 8:10–11). The star called wormwood falls on one third of the rivers, and many men die because the waters are made bitter.					

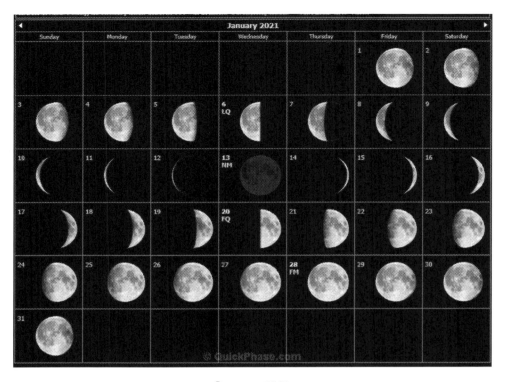

January 2021

February 2021 (Jewish Year 5781)						
Sunday	Monday	Tuesday	Wednesday	Thursday	Friday	Saturday
	1 Sh'vat 18 491	2 Sh'vat 19 492	3 Sh'vat 20 493	4 Sh'vat 21 494	5 Sh'vat 22 495	6 Sh'vat 23 496
7 Sh'vat 24 497	8 Sh'vat 25 498	9 Sh'vat 26 499	10 Sh'vat 27 500	11 Sh'vat 28 501	12 Sh'vat 29 502	13 Sh'vat 30 503
14 Adar 1 504	15 Adar 2 505	16 Adar3 506	17 Adar 4 507	18 Adar 5 508	19 Adar 6 509	20 Adar 7 510
21 Adar 8 511	22 Adar 9 512	23 Adar 10 513	24 Adar 11 514	25 Adar 12 515	26 Adar 13 516	27 Adar 14 517
28 Adar 15 518	Adar is the twelfth month of the Jewish calendar and has twenty-nine days. *February 14*: Sounding of the fourth trumpet (Rev. 8:12).					

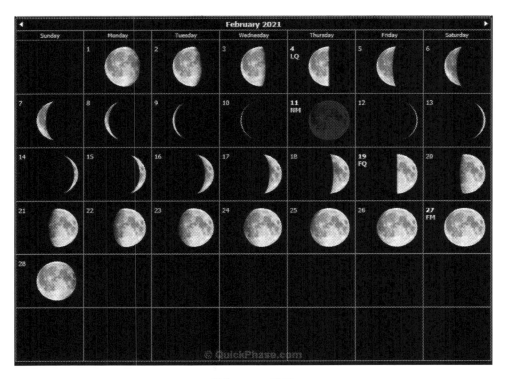

February 2021

"And the fourth angel sounded, and the third part of the sun was smitten, and the third part of the moon, and the third part of the stars; so, as the third part of them was darkened, and the day shone not for a third part of it, and the night likewise" (Rev. 8:12).

March 2021 (Jewish Year 5781)						
Sunday	Monday	Tuesday	Wednesday	Thursday	Friday	Saturday
	1 Adar 16 **519**	**2** Adar 17 **520**	**3** Adar 18 **521**	**4** Adar 19 **522**	**5** Adar 20 **523**	**6** Adar 21 **524**
7 Adar 22 **525**	**8** Adar 23 **526**	**9** Adar 24 **527**	**10** Adar 25 **528**	**11** Adar 26 **529**	**12** Adar 27 **530**	**13** Adar 28 **531**
14 Adar 29 **532**	**15** Nisan 1 **533**	**16** Nisan 2 **534**	**17** Nisan 3 **535**	**18** Nisan 4 **536**	**19** Nisan 5 **537**	**20** Nisan 6 **538**
21 Nisan 7 **539**	**22** Nisan 8 **540**	**23** Nisan 9 **541**	**24** Nisan 10 **542**	**25** Nisan 11 **543**	**26** Nisan 12 **544**	**27** Nisan 13 **545**
28 Nisan 14 **546**	**29** Nisan 15 **547**	**30** Nisan 16 **548**	**31** Nisan 17 **549**	*Nisan 1*: Sounding of fifth trumpet (Rev. 9:1–11). Locusts for five months.		

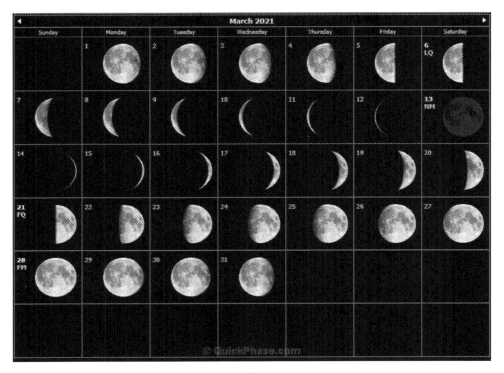

March 2021

March 14: Adar 29 ends at sunset (5:49 p.m.) and starts the month of Nisan.

Nisan 1: Sounding of fifth trumpet (Rev. 9:1–11). There are locusts for five months.

April 2021 (Jewish Year 5781)						
Sunday	Monday	Tuesday	Wednesday	Thursday	Friday	Saturday
				1 Nisan 18 **550**	**2** Nisan 19 **551**	**3** Nisan 20 **552**
4 Nisan 21 **553**	**5** Nisan 22 **554**	**6** Nisan 23 **555**	**7** Nisan 24 **556**	**8** Nisan 25 **557**	**9** Nisan 26 **558**	**10** Nisan 27 **559**
11 Nisan 28 **560**	**12** Nisan 29 **561**	**13** Nisan 30 **562**	**14** Lyyar 1 **563**	**15** Lyyar 2 **564**	**16** Lyyar 3 **565**	**17** Lyyar 4 **566**
18 Lyyar 5 **567**	**19** Lyyar 6 **568**	**20** Lyyar 7 **569**	**21** Lyyar 8 **570**	**22** Lyyar 9 **571**	**23** Lyyar 10 **572**	**24** Lyyar 11 **573**
25 Lyyar 12 **574**	**26** Lyyar 13 **575**	**27** Lyyar 14 **576**	**28** Lyyar 15 **577**	**29** Lyyar 16 **578**	**30** Lyyar 17 **579**	

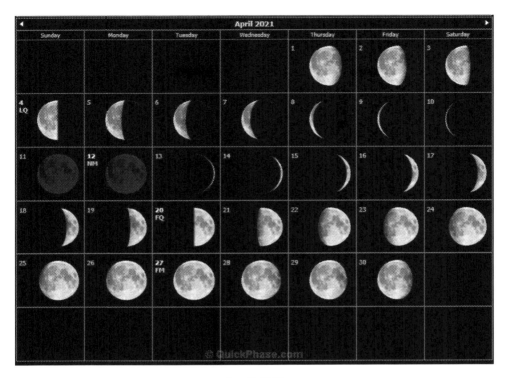

April 2021

Rosh Chodesh Lyyar

April 13: Nisan 30 ends at sunset (6:10 p.m.) and starts the month of Lyyar.

April 14: Lyyar 1 goes until sunset. Lyyar is the second month of the Jewish year and has twenty-nine days.

May 2021 (Jewish Year 5781)						
Sunday	Monday	Tuesday	Wednesday	Thursday	Friday	Saturday
May 11: Yom Yerushalayim, the fifty-fourth anniversary of Israel reclaiming the Holy City (Jerusalem).						**1** Lyyar 18 **580**
2 Lyyar 19 **581**	**3** Lyyar 20 **582**	**4** Lyyar 21 **583**	**5** Lyyar 22 **584**	**6** Lyyar 23 **585**	**7** Lyyar 24 **586**	**8** Lyyar 25 **587**
9 Lyyar 26 **588**	**10** Lyyar 27 **589**	**11** Lyyar 28 **590**	**12** Lyyar 29 **591**	**13** Sivan 1 **592**	**14** Sivan 2 **593**	**15** Sivan 3 **594**
16 Sivan 4 **595**	**17** Sivan 5 **596**	**18** Sivan 6 **597**	**19** Sivan 7 **598**	**20** Sivan 8 **599**	**21** Sivan 9 **600**	**22** Sivan 10 **601**
23 Sivan 11 **602**	**24** Sivan 12 **603**	**25** Sivan 13 **604**	**26** Sivan 14 **605**	**27** Sivan 15 **606**	**28** Sivan 16 **607**	**29** Sivan 17 **608**
30 Sivan 18 **609**	**31** Sivan 19 **610**	Sivan is the third month on the Jewish calendar and has thirty days.				

Rosh Chodesh Sivan

May 12: Lyyar 29 ends at sunset (6:32 p.m.) and begins Sivan 1.

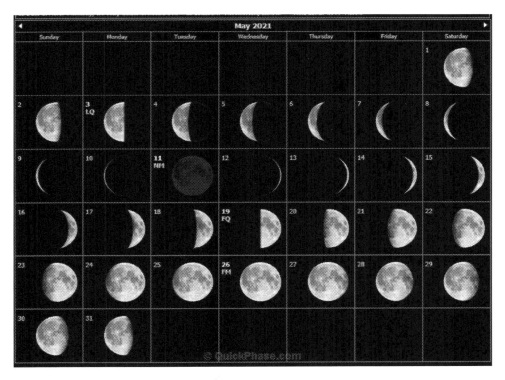

May 2021

June 2021 (Jewish Year 5781)						
Sunday	Monday	Tuesday	Wednesday	Thursday	Friday	Saturday
		1 Sivan 20 **611**	2 Sivan 21 **612**	3 Sivan 22 **613**	4 Sivan 23 **614**	5 Sivan 24 **615**
6 Sivan 25 **616**	7 Sivan 26 **617**	8 Sivan 27 **618**	9 Sivan 28 **619**	10 Sivan 29 **620**	11 Sivan 30 **621**	12 Tamuz 1 **622**
13 Tamuz 2 **623**	14 Tamuz 3 **624**	15 Tamuz 4 **625**	16 Tamuz 5 **626**	17 Tamuz 6 **627**	18 Tamuz 7 **628**	19 Tamuz 8 **629**
20 Tamuz 9 **630**	21 Tamuz 10 **631**	22 Tamuz 11 **632**	23 Tamuz 12 **633**	24 Tamuz 13 **634**	25 Tamuz 14 **635**	26 Tamuz 15 **636**
27 Tamuz 16 **637**	28 Tamuz 17 **638**	29 Tamuz 18 **639**	30 Tamuz 19 **640**	Tamuz is the fourth month on the Jewish calendar and has twenty-nine days.		

Rosh Chodesh Tamuz

June 11: Sivan 30 ends at sunset (6:50 p.m.) and begins Tamuz 1.

June 12: Tamuz 1 ends at sunset. Tamuz is the fourth month on the Jewish calendar and has twenty-nine days.

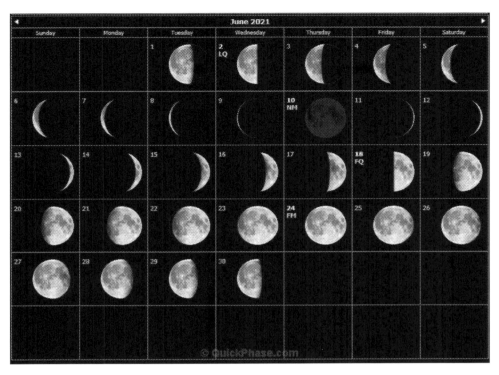

June 2021

July 2021 (Jewish Year 5781)						
Sunday	Monday	Tuesday	Wednesday	Thursday	Friday	Saturday
Av is the fifth month on the Jewish calendar and has thirty days.				1 Tamuz 20 641	2 Tamuz 21 642	3 Tamuz 22 643
4 Tamuz 23 644	5 Tamuz 24 645	6 Tamuz 25 646	7 Tamuz 26 647	8 Tamuz 27 648	9 Tamuz 28 649	10 Tamuz 29 650
11 Av 1 651	12 Av 2 652	13 Av 3 653	14 Av 4 654	15 Av 5 655	16 Av 6 656	17 Av 7 657
18 Av 8 658	19 Av 9 659	20 Av 10 660	21 Av 11 661	22 Av 12 662	23 Av 13 663	24 Av 14 664
25 Av 15 665	26 Av 16 666	27 Av 17 667	28 Av 18 668	29 Av 19 669	30 Av 20 670	31 Av 21 671

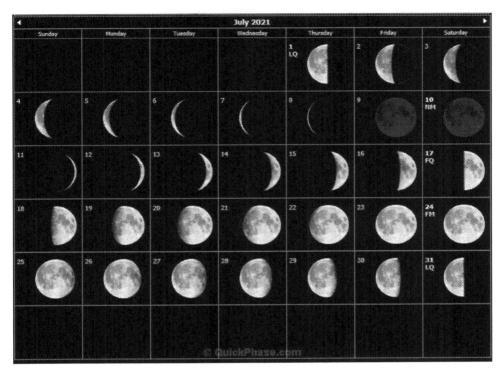

July 2021>

Rosh Chodesh Av

July 10: Tamuz 29 ends at sunset (6:53 p.m.) and begins Av 1.

July 11: Av 1 ends at sunset.

August 2021 (Jewish Year 5781)						
Sunday	Monday	Tuesday	Wednesday	Thursday	Friday	Saturday
1 Av 22 672	2 Av 23 673	3 Av 24 674	4 Av 25 675	5 Av 26 676	6 Av 27 677	7 Av 28 678
8 Av 29 679	9 Av 30 680	10 Elul 1 681	11 Elul 2 682	12 Elul 3 683	13 Elul 4 684	14 Elul 5 685
15 Elul 6 686	16 Elul 7 687	17 Elul 8 688	18 Elul 9 689	19 Elul 10 690	20 Elul 11 691	21 Elul 12 692
22 Elul 13 693	23 Elul 14 694	24 Elul 15 695	25 Elul 16 696	26 Elul 17 697	27 Elul 18 698	28 Elul 19 699
29 Elul 20 700	30 Elul 21 701	31 Elul 22 702	Av 30: End of the locusts of the fifth trumpet (Rev. 9:1–11)			

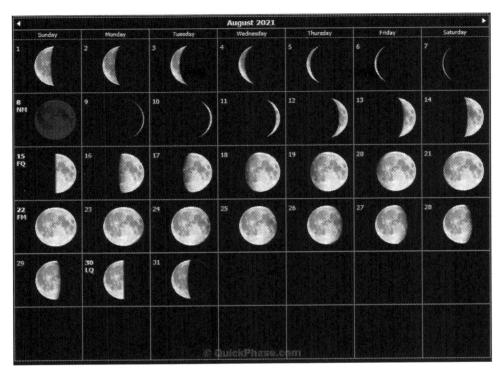

August 2021

Rosh Chodesh Elul

August 9: Av 30 ends at sunset (6:33 p.m.) and begins Elul 1.

August 10: Elul 1 ends at sunset. Elul is the sixth month on the Jewish calendar and has twenty-nine days.

Av 30: End of the locusts of the fifth trumpet (Rev. 9:1–11).

September 2021 (Jewish Year 5781/5782)						
Sunday	Monday	Tuesday	Wednesday	Thursday	Friday	Saturday
Tishri is the seventh month on the Jewish calendar and has thirty days.			**1** Elul 23 703	**2** Elul 24 704	**3** Elul 25 705	**4** Elul 26 706
5 Elul 27 707	**6** Elul 28 708	**7** Elul 29 Sixth trumpet sounds 709	**8** Tishri 1 Feast of Trumpets 710	**9** Tishri 2 711	**10** Tishri 3 712	**11** Tishri 4 713
12 Tishri 5 714	**13** Tishri 6 715	**14** Tishri 7 716	**15** Tishri 8 717	**16** Tishri 9 718	**17** Tishri 10 719	**18** Tishri 11 720
19 Tishri 12 721	**20** Tishri 13 722	**21** Tishri 14 723	**22** Tishri 15 724	**23** Tishri 16 725	**24** Tishri 17 726	**25** Tishri 18 727
26 Tishri 19 728	**27** Tishri 20 729	**28** Tishri 21 730	**29** Tishri 22 731	**30** Tishri 23 732		

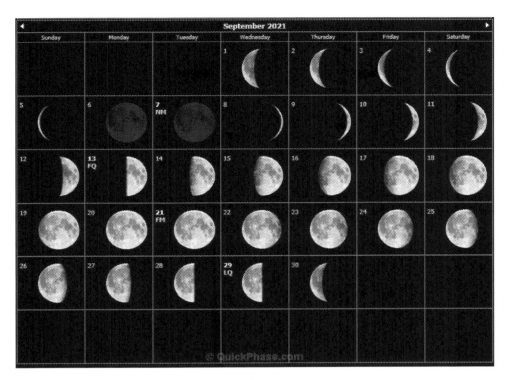

September 2021

Rosh Hashanah

Feast of Trumpets

Tishri 1: Sounding of the sixth trumpet (Rev. 9:14–18). Four angels will be bound in the Euphrates, controlling two hundred million horsemen. One third of men will be killed. Length of time will be one year, one month, one day, one hour.

September 7 (6:00 p.m.): JD 2459465.25

October 2021 (Jewish Year 5782)						
Sunday	**Monday**	Tuesday	Wednesday	Thursday	Friday	Saturday
Revelation 10:7: "But in the days of the voice of the seventh angel, when he shall begin to sound, the mystery of God should be finished, as he hath declared to his servants the prophets."					1 Tishri 24 733	2 Tishri 25 734
3 Tishri 26 735	4 Tishri 27 736	5 Tishri 28 737	6 Tishri 29 738	7 Tishri 30 739	8 Cheshvan 1 740	9 Cheshvan 2 741
10 Cheshvan 3 742	11 Cheshvan 4 743	12 Cheshvan 5 744	13 Cheshvan 6 745	14 Cheshvan 7 746	15 Cheshvan 8 747	16 Cheshvan 9 748
17 Cheshvan 10 749	18 Cheshvan 11 750	19 Cheshvan 12 751	20 Cheshvan 13 752	21 Cheshvan 14 753	22 Cheshvan 15 754	23 Cheshvan 16 755
24 Cheshvan 17 756	25 Cheshvan 18 757	26 Cheshvan 19 758	27 Cheshvan 20 759	28 Cheshvan 21 760	29 Cheshvan 22 761	30 Cheshvan 23 762
31 Cheshvan 24 763	Cheshvan is the eighth month on the Jewish calendar and has twenty-nine or thirty days.					

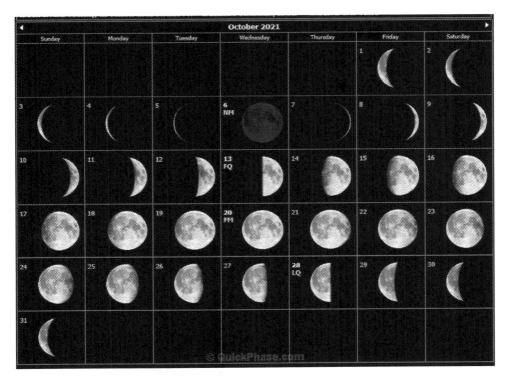

October 2021

Rosh Chodesh Cheshvan

October 7: Tishri 30 ends at sunset (5:18 p.m.) and begins Cheshvan 1.

October 8: Cheshvan 1 ends at sunset. Cheshvan is the eighth month on the Jewish calendar and has twenty-nine or thirty days.

November 2021 (Jewish Year 5782)						
Sunday	Monday	Tuesday	Wednesday	Thursday	Friday	Saturday
	1 Cheshvan 25 764	**2** Cheshvan 26 765	**3** Cheshvan 27 766	**4** Cheshvan 28 767	**5** Cheshvan 29 768	**6** Kislev 1 769
7 Kislev 2 770	**8** Kislev 3 771	**9** Kislev 4 772	**10** Kislev 5 773	**11** Kislev 6 774	**12** Kislev 7 775	**13** Kislev 8 776
14 Kislev 9 777	**15** Kislev 10 778	**16** Kislev 11 779	**17** Kislev 12 780	**18** Kislev 13 781	**19** Kislev 14 782	**20** Kislev 15 783
21 Kislev 16 784	**22** Kislev 17 785	**23** Kislev 18 786	**24** Kislev 19 787	**25** Kislev 20 788	**26** Kislev 21 789	**27** Kislev 22 790
28 Kislev 23 791	**29** Kislev 24 792	**30** Kislev 25 793	Kislev is the ninth month on the Jewish calendar and has thirty days.			

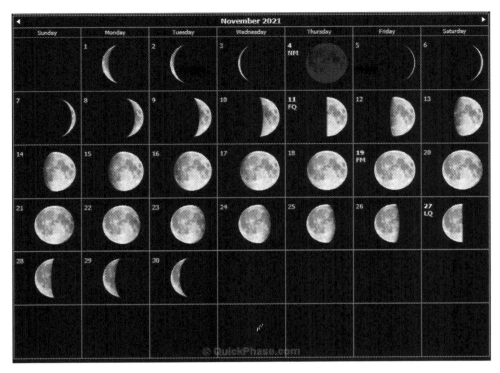

November 2021

Rosh Chodesh Kislev

November 5: Cheshvan 29 ends at sunset (4:47 p.m.) and begins Kislev 1.

November 6: Kislev 1 ends at sunset on November 6. Kislev is the ninth month on the Jewish calendar.

December 2021 (Jewish Year 5781)						
Sunday	**Monday**	**Tuesday**	**Wednesday**	**Thursday**	**Friday**	**Saturday**
Tevet is the tenth month on the Jewish calendar and has twenty-nine days.			1 Kislev 26 794	2 Kislev 27 795	3 Kislev 28 796	4 Kislev 29 797
5 Kislev 30 798	6 Tevet 1 799	7 Tevet 2 800	8 Tevet 3 801	9 Tevet 4 802	10 Tevet 5 803	11 Tevet 6 804
12 Tevet 7 805	13 Tevet 8 806	14 Tevet 9 807	15 Tevet 10 808	16 Tevet 11 809	17 Tevet 12 810	18 Tevet 13 811
19 Tevet 14 812	20 Tevet 15 813	21 Tevet 16 814	22 Tevet 17 815	23 Tevet 18 816	24 Tevet 19 817	25 Tevet 20 818
26 Tevet 21 819	27 Tevet 22 820	28 Tevet 23 821	29 Tevet 24 822	30 Tevet 25 823	31 Tevet 26 824	

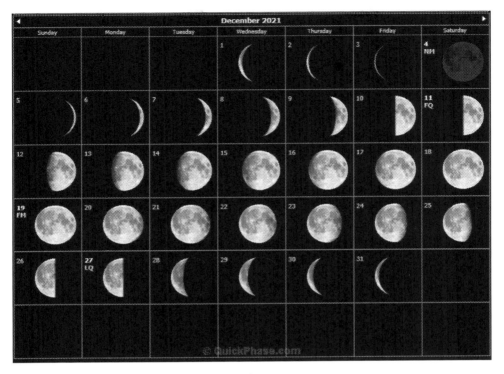

December 2021

Rosh Chodesh Tevet

January 2022 (Jewish Year 5782)						
Sunday	Monday	Tuesday	Wednesday	Thursday	Friday	Saturday
						1 Tevet 27 825
2 Tevet 28 826	**3** Tevet 29 827	**4** Sh'vat 1 828	**5** Sh'vat 2 829	**6** Sh'vat 3 830	**7** Sh'vat 4 831	**8** Sh'vat 5 832
9 Sh'vat 6 833	**10** Sh'vat 7 834	**11** Sh'vat 8 835	**12** Sh'vat 9 836	**13** Sh'vat 10 837	**14** Sh'vat 11 838	**15** Sh'vat 12 839
16 Sh'vat 13 840	**17** Sh'vat 14 841	**18** Sh'vat 15 842	**19** Sh'vat 16 843	**20** Sh'vat 17 844	**21** Sh'vat 18 845	**22** Sh'vat 19 846
23 Sh'vat 20 847	**24** Sh'vat 21 848	**25** Sh'vat 22 849	**26** Sh'vat 23 850	**27** Sh'vat 24 851	**28** Sh'vat 25 852	**29** Sh'vat 26 853
30 Sh'vat 27 854	**31** Sh'vat 28 855					

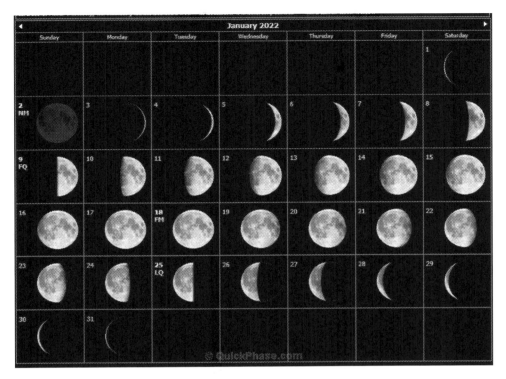

January 2022

Rosh Chodesh Sh'vat

January 3: Tevet 29 ends at sunset (4:47 p.m.) and begins Sh'vat 1.

January 4: Sh'vat 1 ends at sunset. Sh'vat is the eleventh month on the Jewish calendar and has thirty days.

February 2022 (Jewish Year 5782)						
Sunday	Monday	Tuesday	Wednesday	Thursday	Friday	Saturday
		1 Sh'vat 29 **856**	**2** Sh'vat 30 **857**	**3** Adar I 1 **858**	**4** Adar I 2 **859**	**5** Adar I 3 **860**
6 Adar I 4 **861**	**7** Adar I 5 **862**	**8** Adar I 6 **863**	**9** Adar I 7 **864**	**10** Adar I 8 **865**	**11** Adar I 9 **866**	**12** Adar I 10 **867**
13 Adar I 11 **868**	**14** Adar I 12 **869**	**15** Adar I 13 **870**	**16** Adar I 14 **871**	**17** Adar I 15 **872**	**18** Adar I 16 **873**	**19** Adar I 17 **874**
20 Adar I 18 **875**	**21** Adar I 19 **876**	**22** Adar I 20 **877**	**23** Adar I 21 **878**	**24** Adar I 22 **879**	**25** Adar I 23 **880**	**26** Adar I 24 **881**
27 Adar I 25 **882**	**28** Adar I 26 **883**	*February 2*: Sh'vat 30 ends at sunset (5:14 p.m.) and begins Adar I 1. *February 3*: Adar I 1 ends at sunset on February 3. Adar I is a leap month of thirty days and will be followed by Adar II. Adar II is the last month of the year and is twenty-nine days.				

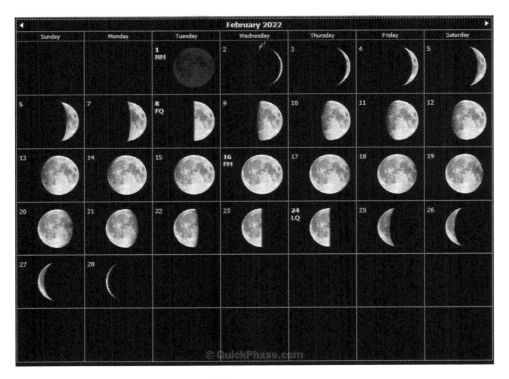

February 2022

Rosh Chodesh Adar 1

February 2: Sh'vat 30 ends at sunset (5:14 p.m.) and begins Adar I 1.

February 3: Adar I 1 ends at sunset. Adar I is a leap month of thirty days and will be followed by Adar II. Adar II is the last month of the year and is twenty-nine days.

March 2022 (Jewish Year 5782)						
Sunday	Monday	Tuesday	Wednesday	Thursday	Friday	Saturday
March 4: Adar I 30 ends at sunset (5:41 p.m.) and begins Adar II 1.		1 Adar I 27 884	2 Adar I 28 885	3 Adar I 29 886	4 Adar I 30 887	5 Adar II 1 888
6 Adar II 2 889	7 Adar II 3 890	8 Adar II 4 891	9 Adar II 5 892	10 Adar II 6 893	11 Adar II 7 894	12 Adar II 8 895
13 Adar II 9 896	14 Adar II 10 897	15 Adar II 11 898	16 Adar II 12 899	17 Adar II 13 900	18 Adar II 14 901	19 Adar II 15 902
20 Adar II 16 903	21 Adar II 17 904	22 Adar II 18 905	23 Adar II 19 906	24 Adar II 20 907	25 Adar II 21 908	26 Adar II 22 909
27 Adar II 23 910	28 Adar II 24 911	29 Adar II 25 912	30 Adar II 26 913	31 Adar II 27 914	*March 5*: Adar II 1 ends at sunset on March 5. Adar II is the twelfth month on the Jewish calendar.	

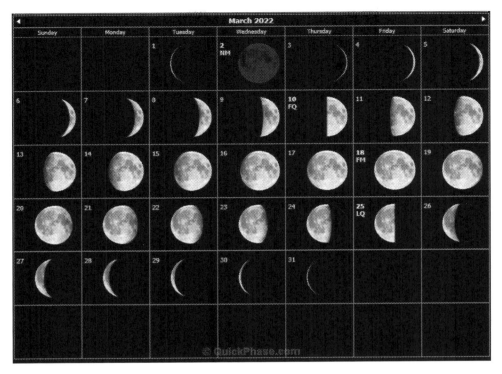

March 2022

Rosh Chodesh Adar II

April 2022 (Jewish Year 5782)						
Sunday	Monday	Tuesday	Wednesday	Thursday	Friday	Saturday
					1 Adar II 28 **915**	**2** Adar II 29 **916**
3 Nisan 1 **917**	**4** Nisan 2 **918**	**5** Nisan 3 **919**	**6** Nisan 4 **920**	**7** Nisan 5 **921**	**8** Nisan 6 **922**	**9** Nisan 7 **923**
10 Nisan 8 **924**	**11** Nisan 9 **925**	**12** Nisan 10 **926**	**13** Nisan 11 **927**	**14** Nisan 12 **928**	**15** Nisan 13 **929**	**16** Nisan 14 **930**
17 Nisan 15 **931**	**18** Nisan 16 **932**	**19** Nisan 17 **933**	**20** Nisan 18 **934**	**21** Nisan 19 **935**	**22** Nisan 20 **936**	**23** Nisan 21 **937**
24 Nisan 22 **938**	**25** Nisan 23 **939**	**26** Nisan 24 **940**	**27** Nisan 25 **941**	**28** Nisan 26 **942**	**29** Nisan 27 **943**	30 Nisan 28 **944**

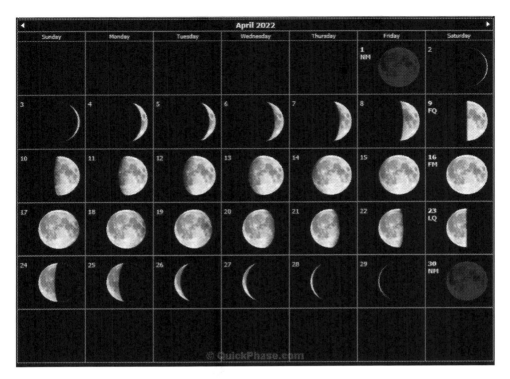

April 2022

Rosh Chodesh Nisan

April 2: Adar II 29 ends at sunset (6:02 p.m.) and begins Nisan 1.

April 3: Nisan 1 ends at sunset. Nisan is the first month on the Jewish calendar and has thirty days.

May 2022 (Jewish Year 5782)						
Sunday	Monday	Tuesday	Wednesday	Thursday	Friday	Saturday
1 Nisan 29 945	2 Nisan 30 946	3 Lyyar 1 947	4 Lyyar 2 948	5 Lyyar 3 949	6 Lyyar 4 950	7 Lyyar 5 951
8 Lyyar 6 952	9 Lyyar 7 953	10 Lyyar 8 954	11 Lyyar 9 955	12 Lyyar 10 956	13 Lyyar 11 957	14 Lyyar 12 958
15 Lyyar 13 959	16 Lyyar 14 960	17 Lyyar 15 961	18 Lyyar 16 962	19 Lyyar 17 963	20 Lyyar 18 964	21 Lyyar 19 965
22 Lyyar 20 966	23 Lyyar 21 967	24 Lyyar 22 968	25 Lyyar 23 969	26 Lyyar 24 970	27 Lyyar 25 971	28 Lyyar 26 972
29 Lyyar 27 973	30 Lyyar 28 974	31 Lyyar 29 975	Lyyar is the second month on the Jewish calendar and has twenty-nine days.			

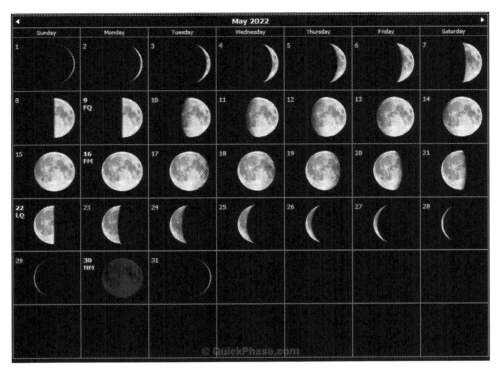

May 2022

Rosh Chodesh Lyyar

May 2: Nisan 30 ends at sunset (6:24 p.m.) and begins Lyyar 1.

May 3: Lyyar 1 ends at sunset on May 3. Lyyar is the second month on the Jewish calendar and has twenty-nine days.

Rosh Chodesh Sivan

May 30: Yom Yerushalayim is the fifty-fifth anniversary of Israel reclaiming the Holy City (Jerusalem).

May 31: Lyyar 29 ends at sunset and starts Sivan 1.

June 1: Sivan 1 ends at sunset. Sivan is the third month of the Jewish calendar and has thirty days.

June 2022 (Jewish Year 5782)						
Sunday	Monday	Tuesday	Wednesday	Thursday	Friday	Saturday
Sivan is the third month of the Jewish calendar and has thirty days			1 Sivan 1 976	2 Sivan 2 977	3 Sivan 3 978	4 Sivan 4 979
5 Sivan 5 980	6 Sivan 6 981	7 Sivan 7 982	8 Sivan 8 983	9 Sivan 9 984	10 Sivan 10 985	11 Sivan 11 986
12 Sivan 12 987	13 Sivan 13 988	14 Sivan 14 989	15 Sivan 15 990	16 Sivan 16 991	17 Sivan 17 992	18 Sivan 18 993
19 Sivan 19 994	20 Sivan 20 995	21 Sivan 21 996	22 Sivan 22 997	23 Sivan 23 998	24 Sivan 24 999	25 Sivan 25 1000
26 Sivan 26 1001	27 Sivan 27 1002	28 Sivan 28 1003	29 Sivan 29 1004	30 Sivan 30 1005		

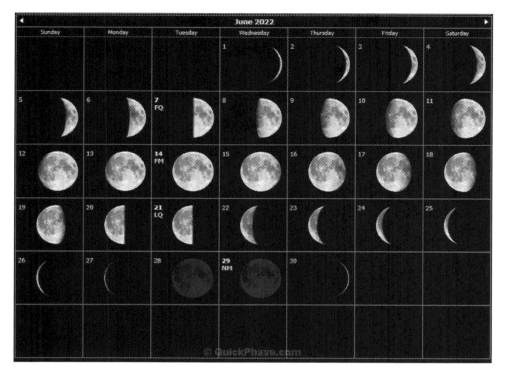

June 2022

Rosh Chodesh Sivan

May 31: Lyyar 29 ends at sunset and starts Sivan 1.

June 1: Sivan 1 ends at sunset. Sivan is the third month of the Jewish calendar and has thirty days.

Rosh Chodesh Tamuz

June 30: Sivan 30 ends at sunset (6:54 p.m.) and starts Tamuz 1.

July 2022 (Jewish Year 5782)						
Sunday	Monday	Tuesday	Wednesday	Thursday	Friday	Saturday
					1 Tamuz 1 **1006**	**2** Tamuz 2 **1007**
3 Tamuz 3 **1008**	**4** Tamuz 4 **1009**	**5** Tamuz 5 **1010**	**6** Tamuz 6 **1011**	**7** Tamuz 7 **1012**	**8** Tamuz 8 **1013**	**9** Tamuz 9 **1014**
10 Tamuz 10 **1015**	**11** Tamuz 11 **1016**	**12** Tamuz 12 **1017**	**13** Tamuz 13 **1018**	**14** Tamuz 14 **1019**	**15** Tamuz 15 **1020**	**16** Tamuz 16 **1021**
17 Tamuz 17 **1022**	**18** Tamuz 18 **1023**	**19** Tamuz 19 **1024**	**20** Tamuz 20 **1025**	**21** Tamuz 21 **1026**	**22** Tamuz 22 **1027**	**23** Tamuz 23 **1028**
24 Tamuz 24 **1029**	**25** Tamuz 25 **1030**	**26** Tamuz 26 **1031**	**27** Tamuz 27 **1032**	**28** Tamuz 28 **1033**	**29** Tamuz 29 **1034**	**30** Av 1 **1035**
31 Av 2 **1036**	Tamuz is the fourth month of the Jewish calendar and has twenty-nine days.					

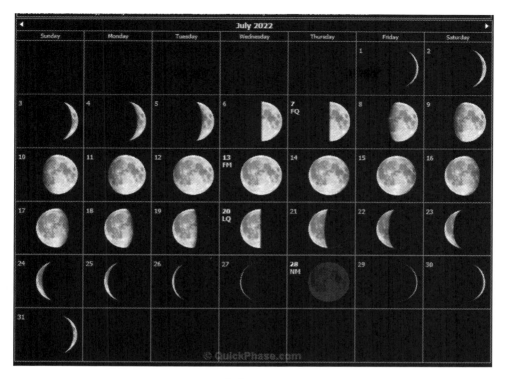

July 2022

Rosh Chodesh Av

July 29: Tamuz 29 ends at sunset (6:43 p.m.) and begins Av 1.

August 2022 (Jewish Year 5782)						
Sunday	Monday	Tuesday	Wednesday	Thursday	Friday	Saturday
	1 Av 3 1037	2 Av 4 1038	3 Av 5 1039	4 Av 6 1040	5 Av 7 1041	6 Av 8 1042
7 Av 9 1043	8 Av 10 1044	9 Av 11 1045	10 Av 12 1046	11 Av 13 1047	12 Av 14 1048	13 Av 15 1049
14 Av 16 1050	15 Av 17 1051	16 Av 18 1052	17 Av 19 1053	18 Av 20 1054	19 Av 21 1055	20 Av 22 1056
21 Av 23 1057	22 Av 24 1058	23 Av 25 1059	24 Av 26 1060	25 Av 27 1061	26 Av 28 1062	27 Av 29 1063
28 Av 30 1064	29 Elul 1 1065	30 Elul 2 1066	31 Elul 3 1067	Av is the fifth month on the Jewish calendar and has thirty days.		

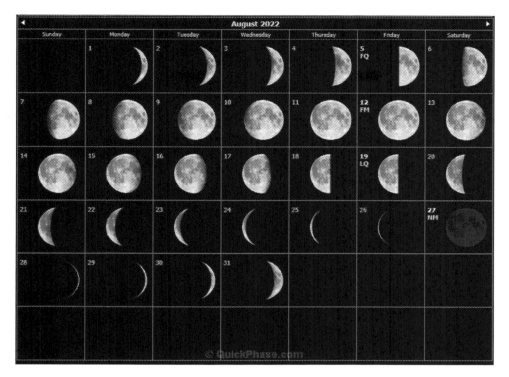

August 2022

Rosh Chodesh Elul

August 28: Av 30 ends at sunset (6:12 p.m.) and begins Elul 1.

August 29: Elul 1 ends at sunset. Elul is the sixth month of the Jewish calendar and has twenty-nine days

September 2022 (Jewish Year 5782/5783)						
Sunday	Monday	Tuesday	Wednesday	Thursday	Friday	Saturday
Elul is the sixth month of the Jewish year and has twenty-nine days. Tishri is the seventh month of the Jewish calendar and has thirty days.				**1** Elul 4 **1068**	**2** Elul 5 **1069**	**3** Elul 6 **1070**
4 Elul 7 **1071**	**5** Elul 8 **1072**	**6** Elul 9 **1073**	**7** Elul 10 **1074**	**8** Elul 11 **1075**	**9** Elul 12 **1076**	**10** Elul 13 **1077**
11 Elul 14 **1078**	**12** Elul 15 **1079**	**13** Elul 16 **1080**	**14** Elul 17 **1081**	**15** Elul 18 **1082**	**16** Elul 19 **1083**	**17** Elul 20 **1084**
18 Elul 21 **1085**	**19** Elul 22 **1086**	**20** Elul 23 **1087**	**21** Elul 24 **1088**	**22** Elul 25 **1089**	**23** Elul 26 **1090**	**24** Elul 27 **1091**
25 Elul 28 **1092**	**26** Elul 29 **1093**	**27** Tishri 1 **1094**	**28** Tishri 2 **1095**	**29** Tishri 3 **1096**	**30** Tishri 4 **1097**	

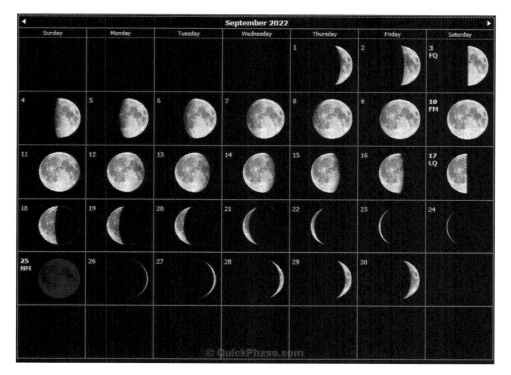

September 2022

September 26: Elul 29 ends at sunset (5:33 p.m.) and starts Tishri 1. It also marks the new year and starts the Feast of Trumpets as recorded in Leviticus 23.

September 27: Tishri 1 ends at sunset (5:33 p.m.). Tishri is the seventh month of the Jewish calendar and has thirty days.

September 27 (4:33 p.m.): End of the sixth trumpet after one year, one month, one day and one hour. The four angels are released from the Euphrates. One third of mankind has been killed.

JD 2459850.189513

October 2022 (Jewish Year 5783)						
Sunday	Monday	Tuesday	Wednesday	Thursday	Friday	Saturday
						1 Tishri 5 **1098**
2 Tishri 6 **1099**	**3** Tishri 7 **1100**	**4** Tishri 8 **1101**	**5** Tishri 9 **1102**	**6** Tishri 10 **1103**	**7** Tishri 11 **1104**	**8** Tishri 12 **1105**
9 Tishri 13 **1106**	**10** Tishri 14 **1107**	**11** Tishri 15 **1108**	**12** Tishri 16 **1109**	**13** Tishri 17 **1110**	**14** Tishri 18 **1111**	**15** Tishri 19 **1112**
16 Tishri 20 **1113**	**17** Tishri 21 **1114**	**18** Tishri 22 **1115**	**19** Tishri 23 **1116**	**20** Tishri 24 **1117**	**21** Tishri 25 **1118**	**22** Tishri 26 **1119**
23 Tishri 27 **1120**	**24** Tishri 28 **1121**	**25** Tishri 29 **1122**	**26** Tishri 30 **1123**	**27** Cheshvan 1 **1124**	**28** Cheshvan 2 **1125**	**29** Cheshvan 3 **1126**
30 Cheshvan 4 **1127**	**31** Cheshvan 5 **1128**	Cheshvan is the eighth month of Jewish calendar and has twenty-nine or thirty days.				

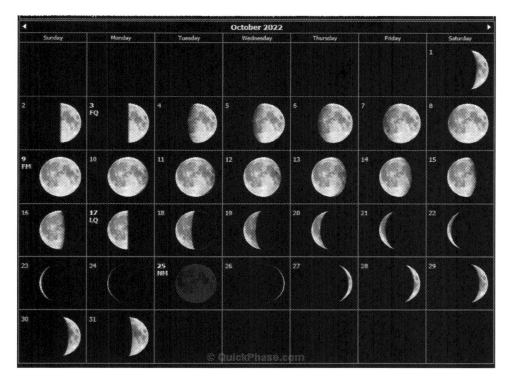

October 2022

October 26: Tishri 30 ends at sunset (4:56 p.m.) and starts Cheshvan 1.

October 27: Cheshvan 1 ends at sunset.

November 2022 (Jewish Year 5783)						
Sunday	Monday	Tuesday	Wednesday	Thursday	Friday	Saturday
		1 Cheshvan 6 **1129**	**2** Cheshvan 7 **1130**	**3** Cheshvan 8 **1131**	**4** Cheshvan 9 **1132**	**5** Cheshvan 10 **1133**
6 Cheshvan 11 **1134**	**7** Cheshvan 12 **1135**	**8** Cheshvan 13 **1136**	**9** Cheshvan 14 **1137**	**10** Cheshvan 15 **1138**	**11** Cheshvan 16 **1139**	**12** Cheshvan 17 **1140**
13 Cheshvan 18 **1141**	**14** Cheshvan 19 **1142**	**15** Cheshvan 20 **1143**	**16** Cheshvan 21 **1144**	**17** Cheshvan 22 **1145**	**18** Cheshvan 23 **1146**	**19** Cheshvan 24 **1147**
20 Cheshvan 25 **1148**	**21** Cheshvan 26 **1149**	**22** Cheshvan 27 **1150**	**23** Cheshvan 28 **1151**	**24** Cheshvan 29 **1152**	**25** Kislev 1 **1153**	**26** Kislev 2 **1154**
27 Kislev 3 **1155**	**28** Kislev 4 **1156**	**29** Kislev 5 **1157**	**30** Kislev 6 **1158**	Kislev is the ninth month of Jewish calendar and has twenty-nine or thirty days.		

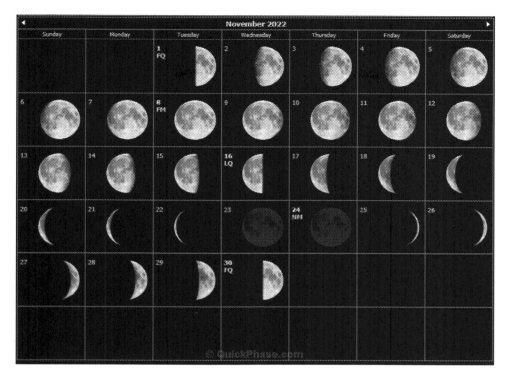

November 2022

November 24: Cheshvan 29 ends at sunset (4:35 p.m.) and begins Kislev 1.

November 25: Kislev 1 ends at sunset. Kislev is the ninth month of Jewish calendar and has twenty-nine or thirty days.

December 2022 (Jewish Year 5783)						
Sunday	Monday	Tuesday	Wednesday	Thursday	Friday	Saturday
Tevet is the tenth month of the Jewish calendar and has twenty-nine days.				1 Kislev 7 1159	2 Kislev 8 1160	3 Kislev 9 1161
4 Kislev 10 1162	5 Kislev 11 1163	6 Kislev 12 1164	7 Kislev 13 1165	8 Kislev 14 1166	9 Kislev 15 1167	10 Kislev 16 1168
11 Kislev 17 1169	12 Kislev 18 1170	13 Kislev 19 1171	14 Kislev 20 1172	15 Kislev 21 1173	16 Kislev 22 1174	17 Kislev 23 1175
18 Kislev 24 1176	19 Kislev 25 1177	20 Kislev 26 1178	21 Kislev 27 1179	22 Kislev 28 1180	23 Kislev 29 1181	24 Kislev 30 1182
25 Tevet 1 1183	26 Tevet 2 1184	27 Tevet 3 1185	28 Tevet 4 1186	29 Tevet 5 1187	30 Tevet 6 1188	31 Tevet 7 1189

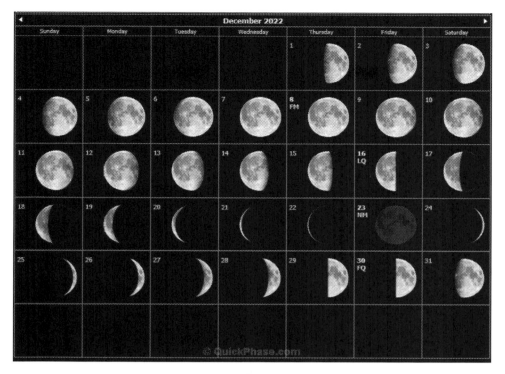

December 2022

December 24: Kislev 30 ends at sunset (4:40 p.m.) and begins Tevet 1.

December 25: Tevet 1 ends at sunset. Tevet is the tenth month of the Jewish calendar and has twenty-nine days.

January 2023 (Jewish Year 5783)						
Sunday	Monday	Tuesday	Wednesday	Thursday	Friday	Saturday
1 Tevet 8 1190	2 Tevet 9 1191	3 Tevet 10 1192	4 Tevet 11 1193	5 Tevet 12 1194	6 Tevet 13 1195	7 Tevet 14 1196
8 Tevet 15 1197	9 Tevet 16 1198	10 Tevet 17 1199	11 Tevet 18 1200	12 Tevet 19 1201	13 Tevet 20 1202	14 Tevet 21 1203
15 Tevet 22 1204	16 Tevet 23 1205	17 Tevet 24 1206	18 Tevet 25 1207	19 Tevet 26 1208	20 Tevet 27 1209	21 Tevet 28 1210
22 Tevet 29 1211	23 Sh'vat 1 1212	24 Sh'vat 2 1213	25 Sh'vat 3 1214	26 Sh'vat 4 1215	27 Sh'vat 5 1216	28 Sh'vat 6 1217
29 Sh'vat 7 1218	30 Sh'vat 8 1219	31 Sh'vat 9 1220	*January 22*: Tevet 29 ends at sunset. Sh'vat is the eleventh month of the Jewish calendar and has thirty days.			

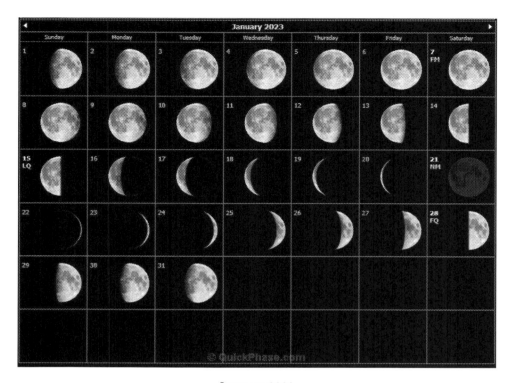

January 2023

Rosh Chodesh Sh'vat

January 22: Tevet 29 ends at sunset (5:05 p.m.) and begins Sh'vat 1.

January 23: Sh'vat 1 ends at sunset. Sh'vat is the eleventh month of the Jewish calendar and has thirty days.

February 2023 (Jewish Year 5783)						
Sunday	Monday	Tuesday	Wednesday	Thursday	Friday	Saturday
			1 Sh'vat 10 **1221**	**2** Sh'vat 11 **1222**	**3** Sh'vat 12 **1223**	**4** Sh'vat 13 **1224**
5 Sh'vat 14 **1225**	**6** Sh'vat 15 **1226**	**7** Sh'vat 16 **1227**	**8** Sh'vat 17 **1228**	**9** Sh'vat 18 **1229**	**10** Sh'vat 19 **1230**	**11** Sh'vat 20 **1231**
12 Sh'vat 21 **1232**	**13** Sh'vat 22 **1233**	**14** Sh'vat 23 **1234**	**15** Sh'vat 24 **1235**	**16** Sh'vat 25 **1236**	**17** Sh'vat 26 **1237**	**18** Sh'vat 27 **1238**
19 Sh'vat 28 **1239**	**20** Sh'vat 29 **1240**	**21** Sh'vat 30 **1241**	**22** Adar 1 **1242**	**23** Adar 2 **1243**	**24** Adar 3 **1244**	**25** Adar 4 **1245**
26 Adar 5 **1246**	**27** Adar 6 **1247**	**28** Adar 7 **1248**	*February 21*: Sh'vat 30 ends at sunset (5:31 p.m.) and starts Adar 1. Adar is the twelfth month of the Jewish calendar and has twenty-nine days.			

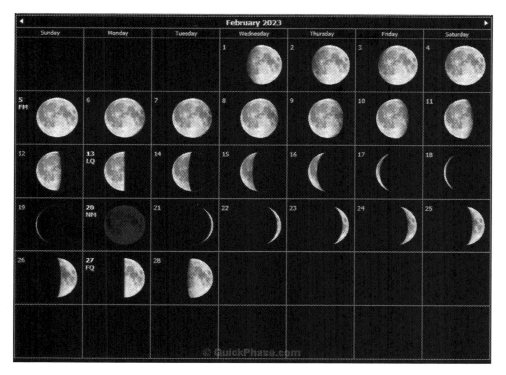

February 2023

February 21: Sh'vat 30 ends at sunset (5:31 p.m.) and starts Adar 1.

February 22: Adar 1 ends at sunset. Adar is the twelfth month of the Jewish calendar and has twenty-nine days.

March 2023 (Jewish Year 5783)						
Sunday	Monday	Tuesday	Wednesday	Thursday	Friday	Saturday
March 12: Antichrist places the abomination of desolation in the temple in Jerusalem, 1,260 days from the signing of the treaty. JD 2460015.5			**1** Adar 8 **1249**	**2** Adar 9 **1250**	**3** Adar 10 **1251**	**4** Adar 11 **1252**
5 Adar 12 **1253**	**6** Adar 13 **1254**	**7** Adar 14 **1255**	**8** Adar 15 **1256**	**9** Adar 16 **1257**	**10** Adar 17 **1258**	**11** Adar 18 **1259**
12 Adar 19 **1260** ___	**13** Adar 20 **001** ___	**14** Adar 21 **002** ___	**15** Adar 22 **003** ___	**16** Adar 23 **004** ___	**17** Adar 24 **005** ___	**18** Adar 25 **006** ___
19 Adar 26 **007** ___	**20** Adar 27 **008** ___	**21** Adar 28 **009** ___	**22** Adar 29 **010** ___	**23** Nisan 1 **011** ___	**24** Nisan 2 **012** ___	**25** Nisan 3 **013** ___
26 Nisan 4 **014** ___	**27** Nisan 5 **015** ___	**28** Nisan 6 **016** ___	**29** Nisan 7 **017** ___	**30** Nisan 8 **018** ___	**31** Nisan 9 **019** ___	

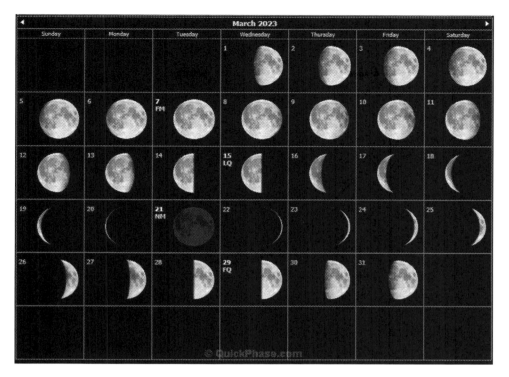

March 2023

March 22: Adar 29 ends at sunset (5:54 p.m.) and begins Nisan 1.

March 23: Nisan 1 ends at sunset. Nisan is the first month of the Jewish year and has thirty days.

April 2023 (Jewish Year 5783)						
Sunday	Monday	Tuesday	Wednesday	Thursday	Friday	Saturday
Nisan is the first month of the Jewish year and has thirty days. April 12: Start date for the last forty-two months (1,260 days).						**1** Nisan 10 **020** ___
2 Nisan 11 **021** ___	**3** Nisan 12 **022** ___	**4** Nisan 13 **023** ___	**5** Nisan 14 **024** ___	**6** Nisan 15 **025** ___	**7** Nisan 16 **026** ___	**8** Nisan 17 **027** ___
9 Nisan 18 **028** ___	**10** Nisan 19 **029** ___	**11** Nisan 20 **030** ___	**12** Nisan 21 **031** **001**	**13** Nisan 22 **032** **002**	**14** Nisan 23 **033** **003**	**15** Nisan 24 **034** **004**
16 Nisan 25 **035** **005**	**17** Nisan 26 **036** **006**	**18** Nisan 27 **037** **007**	**19** Nisan 28 **038** **008**	**20** Nisan 29 **039** **009**	**21** Nisan 30 **040** **010**	**22** Lyyar 1 **041** **011**
23 Lyyar 2 **042** **012**	**24** Lyyar 3 **043** **013**	**25** Lyyar 4 **044** **014**	**26** Lyyar 5 **045** **015**	**27** Lyyar 6 **046** **016**	**28** Lyyar 7 **047** **017**	**29** Lyyar 8 **048** **018**
30 Lyyar 9 **049** **019**	April 12: The Antichrist receives the full power of Satan for forty-two months (Rev. 13:5). Lyyar is the second month of the Jewish calendar and has twenty-nine days.					

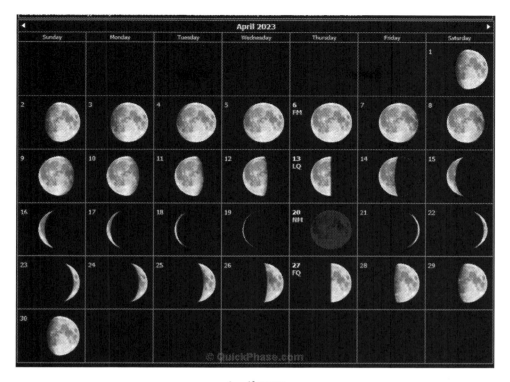

April 2023

Rosh Chodesh Lyyar

April 21: Nisan 30 ends at sunset (6:38 p.m.) and starts Lyyar 1.

April 22: Lyyar 1 ends at sunset. Lyyar is the second month of the Jewish calendar and has twenty-nine days.

May 2023 (Jewish Year 5783)						
Sunday	Monday	Tuesday	Wednesday	Thursday	Friday	Saturday
	1 Lyyar 10 **050** **020**	**2** Lyyar 11 **051** **021**	**3** Lyyar 12 **052** **022**	**4** Lyyar 13 **053** **023**	**5** Lyyar 14 **054** **024**	**6** Lyyar 15 **055** **025**
7 Lyyar 16 **056** **026**	**8** Lyyar 17 **057** **027**	**9** Lyyar 18 **058** **028**	**10** Lyyar 19 **059** **029**	**11** Lyyar 20 **060** **030**	**12** Lyyar 21 **061** **031**	**13** Lyyar 22 **062** **032**
14 Lyyar 23 **063** **033**	**15** Lyyar 24 **064** **034**	**16** Lyyar 25 **065** **035**	**17** Lyyar 26 **066** **036**	**18** Lyyar 27 **067** **037**	**19** Lyyar 28 **068** **038**	**20** Lyyar 29 **069** **039**
21 Sivan 1 **070** **040**	**22** Sivan 2 **071** **041**	**23** Sivan 3 **072** **042**	**24** Sivan 4 **073** **043**	**25** Sivan 5 **074** **044**	**26** Sivan 6 **075** **045**	**27** Sivan 7 **076** **046**
28 Sivan 8 **077** **047**	**29** Sivan 9 **078** **048**	**30** Sivan 10 **079** **049**	**31** Sivan 11 **080** **050**	*May 1*: 42 months (1,240 days) Revelation 13:5 JD 2460066 *May 19*: Yom Yerushalayim is the fifty-sixth anniversary of Israel reclaiming the Holy City (Jerusalem).		

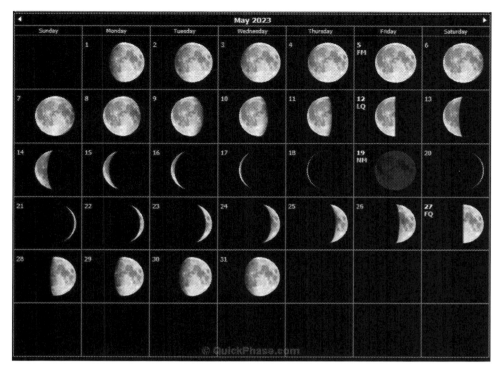

May 2023

Rosh Chodesh Sivan

May 19: Yom Yerushalayim is the fifty-sixth anniversary of Israel reclaiming the Holy City (Jerusalem).

May 20: Lyyar 29 ends at sunset (6:37 p.m.) and begins Sivan 1.

May 21: Sivan 1 ends at sunset. Sivan is the third month of the Jewish calendar and has thirty days.

June 2023 (Jewish Year 5783)						
Sunday	Monday	Tuesday	Wednesday	Thursday	Friday	Saturday
Tamuz is the fourth month of the Jewish year and has twenty-nine days.				**1** Sivan 12 081 051	**2** Sivan 13 082 052	**3** Sivan 14 083 053
4 Sivan 15 084 054	**5** Sivan 16 085 055	**6** Sivan 17 086 056	**7** Sivan 18 087 057	**8** Sivan 19 088 058	**9** Sivan 20 089 059	**10** Sivan 21 090 060
11 Sivan 22 091 061	**12** Sivan 23 092 062	**13** Sivan 24 093 063	**14** Sivan 25 094 064	**15** Sivan 26 095 065	**16** Sivan 27 096 066	**17** Sivan 28 097 067
18 Sivan 29 098 068	**19** Sivan 30 099 069	**20** Tamuz 1 100 070	**21** Tamuz 2 101 071	**22** Tamuz 3 102 072	**23** Tamuz 4 103 073	**24** Tamuz 5 104 074
25 Tamuz 6 105 075	**26** Tamuz 7 106 076	**27** Tamuz 8 107 077	**28** Tamuz 9 108 078	**29** Tamuz 10 109 079	**30** Tamuz 11 110 080	

Rosh Chodesh Tamuz

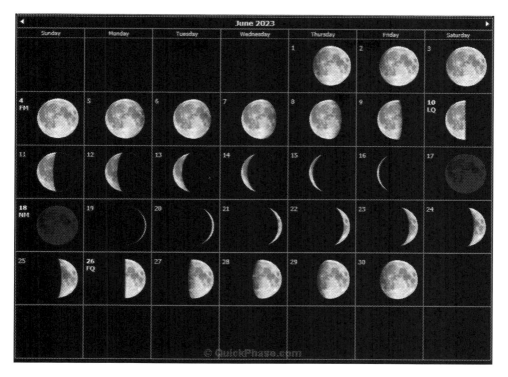

June 2023

June 19: Sivan 30 ends at sunset (6:53 p.m.) and starts Tamuz 1.

June 20: Tamuz 1 ends at sunset. Tamuz is the fourth month of the Jewish year and has twenty-nine days.

July 2023 (Jewish Year 5783)						
Sunday	Monday	Tuesday	Wednesday	Thursday	Friday	Saturday
						1 Tamuz 12 **111** **081**
2 Tamuz 13 **112** **082**	**3** Tamuz 14 **113** **083**	**4** Tamuz 15 **114** **084**	**5** Tamuz 16 **115** **085**	**6** Tamuz 17 **116** **086**	**7** Tamuz 18 **117** **087**	**8** Tamuz 19 **118** **088**
9 Tamuz 20 **119** **089**	**10** Tamuz 21 **120** **090**	**11** Tamuz 22 **121** **091**	**12** Tamuz 23 **122** **092**	**13** Tamuz 24 **123** **093**	**14** Tamuz 25 **124** **094**	**15** Tamuz 26 **125** **095**
16 Tamuz 27 **126** **096**	**17** Tamuz 28 **127** **097**	**18** Tamuz 29 **128** **098**	**19** Av 1 **129** **099**	**20** Av 2 **130** **100**	**21** Av 3 **131** **101**	**22** Av 4 **132** **102**
23 Av 5 **133** **103**	**24** Av 6 **134** **104**	**25** Av 7 **135** **105**	**26** Av 8 **136** **106**	**27** Av 9 **137** **107**	**28** Av 10 **138** **108**	**29** Av 11 **139** **109**
30 Av 12 **140** **110**	**31** Av 13 **141** **111**	Av is the fifth month of Jewish year and has thirty days.				

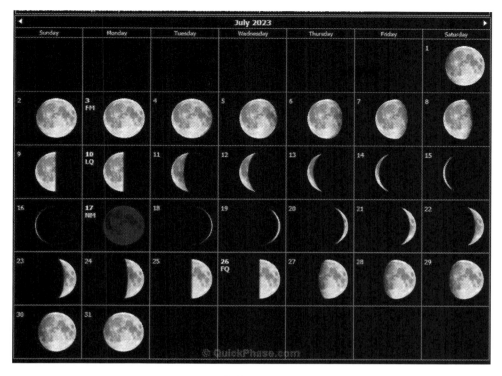

July 2023

Rosh Chodesh Av

July 18: Tamuz 29 ends at sunset (6:50 p.m.) and starts Av 1.

July 19: Av 1 ends at sunset. Av is the fifth month of Jewish year and has thirty days.

August 2023 (Jewish Year 5783)						
Sunday	Monday	Tuesday	Wednesday	Thursday	Friday	Saturday
		1 Av 14 142 112	2 Av 15 143 113	3 Av 16 144 114	4 Av 17 145 115	5 Av 18 146 116
6 Av 19 147 117	7 Av 20 148 118	8 Av 21 149 119	9 Av 22 150 120	10 Av 23 151 121	11 Av 24 152 122	12 Av 25 153 123
13 Av 26 154 124	14 Av 27 155 125	15 Av 28 156 126	16 Av 29 157 127	17 Av 30 158 128	18 Elul 1 159 129	19 Elul 2 160 130
20 Elul 3 161 131	21 Elul 4 162 132	22 Elul 5 163 133	23 Elul 6 164 134	24 Elul 7 165 135	25 Elul 8 166 136	26 Elul 9 167 137
27 Elul 10 168 138	28 Elul 11 169 139	29 Elul 12 170 140	30 Elul 13 171 141	31 Elul 14 172 142	Elul is the sixth month of the Jewish calendar and has twenty-nine days.	

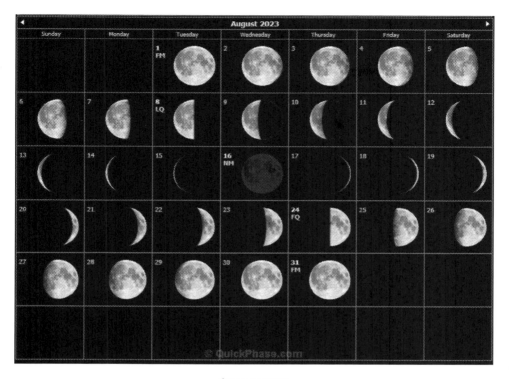

August 2023

August 17: Av 30 ends at sunset (6:25 p.m.) and starts Elul 1.

August 18: Elul 1 ends at sunset. Elul is the sixth month of the Jewish calendar and has twenty-nine days.

September 2023 (Jewish Year 5783/5784)						
Sunday	Monday	Tuesday	Wednesday	Thursday	Friday	Saturday
September 12: Two witnesses killed after 1,260 days and left to lie in the streets for three and a half days (Rev. 11:8). *September 15*: Sounding of the seventh trumpet. JD 2460204					**1** Elul 15 173 143	**2** Elul 16 174 144
3 Elul 17 175 145	**4** Elul 18 176 146	**5** Elul 19 177 147	**6** Elul 20 178 148	**7** Elul 21 179 149	**8** Elul 22 180 150	**9** Elul 23 181 151
10 Elul 24 182 152	**11** Elul 25 183 153	**12** Elul 26 184 154	**13** Elul 27 185 155	**14** Elul 28 186 156	**15** Elul 29 187 157	**16** Tishri 1 188 158
17 Tishri 2 189 159	**18** Tishri 3 190 160	**19** Tishri 4 191 161	**20** Tishri 5 192 162	**21** Tishri 6 193 163	**22** Tishri 7 194 164	**23** Tishri 8 195 165
24 Tishri 9 196 166	**25** Tishri 10 197 167	**26** Tishri 11 198 168	**27** Tishri 12 199 169	**28** Tishri 13 200 170	**29** Tishri 14 201 171	**30** Tishri 15 202 172

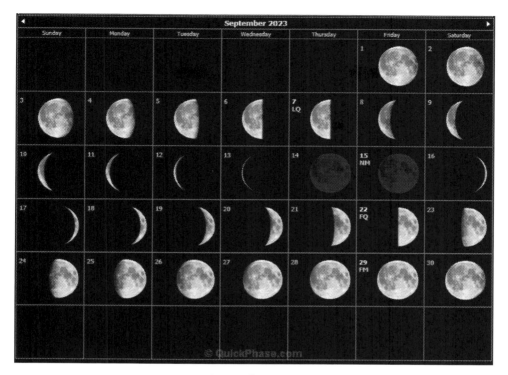

September 2023

September 15: Elul 29 ends at sunset (5:48 p.m.) and begins Tishri 1. Tishri 1 is also known as Rosh Hashanah, which is the start of the Jewish political year.

September 16: Tishri 1 ends at sunset. Tishri is the seventh month of the Jewish calendar.

Rosh Hashana is also called:

- "The Awakening Blast of the Righteous"
- "The Coronation of the Messiah"
- "The Marriage Supper of the Messiah"
- "The Judgement of the Righteous"
- "The Opening of the Books of Judgement"
- "The Day That No Man Knows" (Matthew 24:36, Mark 13: 32)

The Jewish idiom "No man knows the day or hour" is a reference to this day and has been called this for at least 4,000 years.

October 2023 (Jewish Year 5784)						
Sunday	Monday	Tuesday	Wednesday	Thursday	Friday	Saturday
1 Tishri 16 203 173	2 Tishri 17 204 174	3 Tishri 18 205 175	4 Tishri 19 206 176	5 Tishri 20 207 177	6 Tishri 21 208 178	7 Tishri 22 209 179
8 Tishri 23 210 180	9 Tishri 24 211 181	10 Tishri 25 212 182	10 Tishri 26 213 183	12 Tishri 27 214 184	13 Tishri 28 215 185	14 Tishri 29 216 186
15 Tishri 30 217 187	16 Cheshvan 1 218 188	17 Cheshvan 2 219 189	18 Cheshvan 3 220 190	19 Cheshvan 4 221 191	20 Cheshvan 5 222 192	21 Cheshvan 6 223 193
22 Cheshvan 7 224 194	23 Cheshvan 8 225 195	24 Cheshvan 9 226 196	25 Cheshvan 10 227 197	26 Cheshvan 11 228 198	27 Cheshvan 12 229 199	28 Cheshvan 13 230 200
29 Cheshvan 14 231 201	30 Cheshvan 15 232 202	31 Cheshvan 16 233 203	Cheshvan is the eighth month of the Jewish calendar and has twenty-nine or thirty days.			

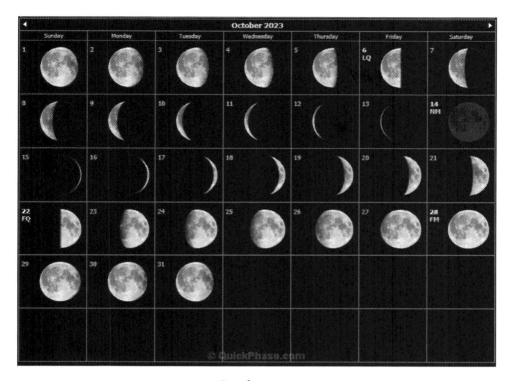

October 2023

October 15: Tishri 30 ends at sunset (5:09 p.m.) and starts Cheshvan 1.

October 16: Cheshvan 1 ends at sunset. Cheshvan is the eighth month of the Jewish calendar and has twenty-nine or thirty days.

November 2023 (Jewish Year 5784)						
Sunday	Monday	Tuesday	Wednesday	Thursday	Friday	Saturday
Kislev 1: First bowl of God's wrath is poured out.			**1** Cheshvan 17 234 204	**2** Cheshvan 18 235 205	**3** Cheshvan 19 236 206	**4** Cheshvan 20 237 207
5 Cheshvan 21 238 208	**6** Cheshvan 22 239 209	**7** Cheshvan 23 240 210	**8** Cheshvan 24 241 211	**9** Cheshvan 25 242 212	**10** Cheshvan 26 243 213	**11** Cheshvan 27 244 214
12 Cheshvan 28 245 215	**13** Cheshvan 29 246 216	**14** Cheshvan 30 247 217	**15** Kislev 1 248 218	**16** Kislev 2 249 219	**17** Kislev 3 250 220	**18** Kislev 4 251 221
19 Kislev 5 252 222	**20** Kislev 6 253 223	**21** Kislev 7 254 224	**22** Kislev 8 255 225	**23** Kislev 9 256 226	**24** Kislev 10 257 227	**25** Kislev 11 258 228
26 Kislev 12 259 229	**27** Kislev 13 260 230	**28** Kislev 14 261 231	**29** Kislev 15 262 232	**30** Kislev 16 263 233		

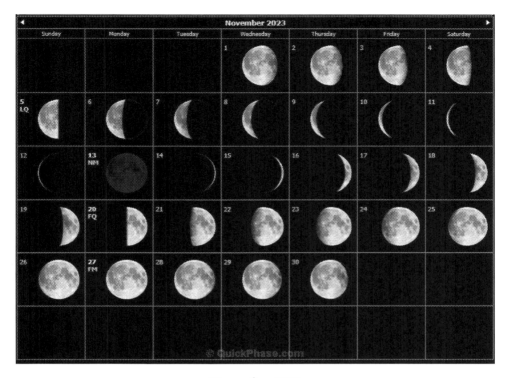

November 2023

November 14: Cheshvan 30 ends at sunset (4:41 p.m.) and starts Kislev 1.

Kislev 1: "And I heard a great voice out of the temple saying to the seven angels, Go your ways, and pour out the vials of the wrath of God upon the earth. And the first went, and poured out his vial upon the earth; and there fell a noisome and grievous sore upon the men which had the mark of the beast, and *upon* them which worshipped his image" (Rev. 16:1–2).

November 15: Kislev 1 ends at sunset. Kislev is the ninth month of the Jewish calendar and has twenty-nine or thirty days.

December 2023 (Jewish Year 5784)						
Sunday	Monday	Tuesday	Wednesday	Thursday	Friday	Saturday
					1 Kislev 17 264 234	**2** Kislev 18 265 235
3 Kislev 19 266 236	**4** Kislev 20 267 237	**5** Kislev 21 268 238	**6** Kislev 22 269 239	**7** Kislev 23 270 240	**8** Kislev 24 271 241	**9** Kislev 25 272 242
10 Kislev 26 273 243	**11** Kislev 27 274 244	**12** Kislev 28 275 245	**13** Kislev 29 276 246	**14** Tevet 1 277 247	**15** Tevet 2 278 248	**16** Tevet 3 279 249
17 Tevet 4 280 250	**18** Tevet 5 281 251	**19** Tevet 6 282 252	**20** Tevet 7 283 253	**21** Tevet 8 284 254	**22** Tevet 9 285 255	**23** Tevet 10 286 256
24 Tevet 11 287 257	**25** Tevet 12 288 258	**26** Tevet 13 289 259	**27** Tevet 14 290 260	**28** Tevet 15 291 261	**29** Tevet 16 292 262	**30** Tevet 17 293 263
31 Tevet 18 294 264						

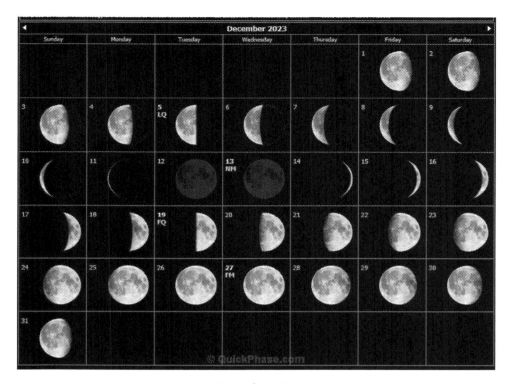

December 2023

Rosh Chodesh Tevet

December 13: Kislev 29 ends at sunset (4:36 p.m.) and starts Tevet 1.

December 14: Tevet 1 ends at sunset. Tevet is the tenth month of the Jewish religious year and has twenty-nine days.

January 2024 (Jewish Year 5784)						
Sunday	Monday	Tuesday	Wednesday	Thursday	Friday	Saturday
	1 Tevet 19 295 265	2 Tevet 20 296 266	3 Tevet 21 297 267	4 Tevet 22 298 268	5 Tevet 23 299 269	6 Tevet 24 300 270
7 Tevet 25 301 271	8 Tevet 26 302 272	9 Tevet 27 303 273	10 Tevet 28 304 274	11 Tevet 29 305 275	12 Sh'vat 1 306 276	13 Sh'vat 2 307 277
14 Sh'vat 3 308 278	15 Sh'vat 4 309 279	16 Sh'vat 5 310 280	17 Sh'vat 6 311 281	18 Sh'vat 7 312 282	19 Sh'vat 8 313 283	20 Sh'vat 9 314 284
21 Sh'vat 10 315 285	22 Sh'vat 11 316 286	23 Sh'vat 12 317 287	24 Sh'vat 13 318 288	25 Sh'vat 14 319 289	26 Sh'vat 15 320 290	27 Sh'vat 16 321 291
28 Sh'vat 17 322 292	29 Sh'vat 18 323 293	30 Sh'vat 19 324 294	31 Sh'vat 20 325 295	Sh'vat is the eleventh month of the Jewish calendar and has thirty days.		

Rosh Chodesh Sh'vat

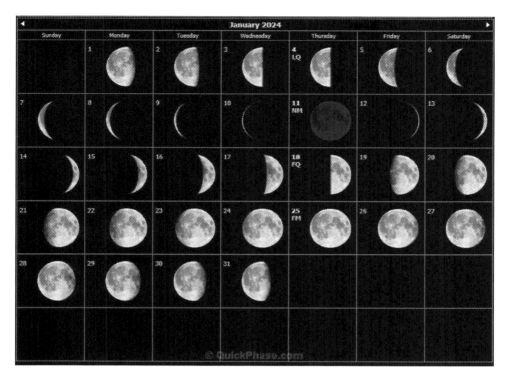

January 2024

January 11: Tevet 29 ends at sunset (4:53 p.m.) and starts Sh'vat 1.

January 12: Sh'vat 1 ends at sunset. Sh'vat is the eleventh month of the Jewish calendar and has thirty days.

February 2024 (Jewish Year 5784)						
Sunday	Monday	Tuesday	Wednesday	Thursday	Friday	Saturday
Adar I is a leap month on the Jewish calendar.				**1** Sh'vat 21 326 296	**2** Sh'vat 22 327 297	**3** Sh'vat 23 328 298
4 Sh'vat 24 329 299	**5** Sh'vat 25 330 300	**6** Sh'vat 26 331 301	**7** Sh'vat 27 332 302	**8** Sh'vat 28 333 303	**9** Sh'vat 29 334 304	**10** Sh'vat 30 335 305
11 Adar I 1 336 306	**12** Adar I 2 337 307	**13** Adar I 3 338 308	**14** Adar I 4 339 309	**15** Adar I 5 340 310	**16** Adar I 6 341 311	**17** Adar I 7 342 312
18 Adar I 8 343 313	**19** Adar I 9 344 314	**20** Adar I 10 345 315	**21** Adar I 11 346 316	**22** Adar I 12 347 317	**23** Adar I 13 348 318	**24** Adar I 14 349 319
25 Adar I 15 350 320	**26** Adar I 16 351 321	**27** Adar I 17 352 322	**28** Adar I 18 353 323	**29** Adar I 19 354 324		

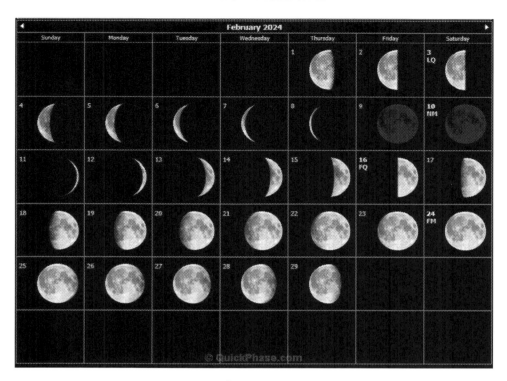

February 2024

March 2024 (Jewish Year 5784)						
Sunday	Monday	Tuesday	Wednesday	Thursday	Friday	Saturday
March 12 (Adar II 1): The second vial of God's wrath poured out.					**1** Adar I 20 355 325	**2** Adar I 21 356 326
3 Adar I 22 357 327	**4** Adar I 23 358 328	**5** Adar I 24 359 329	**6** Adar I 25 360 330	**7** Adar I 26 361 331	**8** Adar I 27 362 332	**9** Adar I 28 363 333
10 Adar I 29 364 334	**11** Adar I 30 365 335	**12** Adar II 1 366 336	**13** Adar II 2 367 337	**14** Adar II 3 368 338	**15** Adar II 4 369 339	**16** Adar II 5 370 340
17 Adar II 6 371 341	**18** Adar II 7 372 342	**19** Adar II 8 373 343	**20** Adar II 9 374 344	**21** Adar II 10 375 345	**22** Adar II 11 376 346	**23** Adar II 12 377 347
24 Adar II 13 378 348	**25** Adar II 14 379 349	**26** Adar II 15 380 350	**27** Adar II 16 381 351	**28** Adar II 17 382 352	**29** Adar II 18 383 353	**30** Adar II 19 384 354
31 Adar II 20 385 355	Adar II is the last month of the Jewish year and has twenty-nine days.					

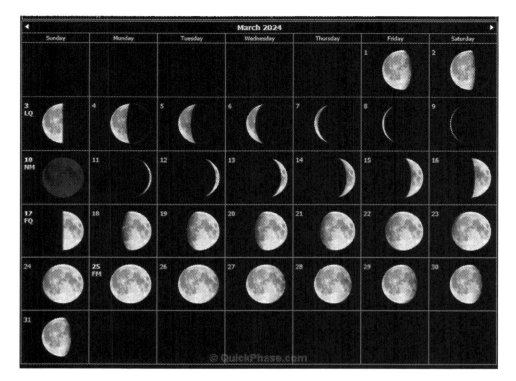

March 2024

March 11: Adar I 30 ends at sunset (5:22 p.m.) and starts Adar II 1.

Adar II 1: "And the second angel poured out his vial upon the sea; and it became as the blood of a dead *man*: and every living soul died in the sea" (Rev. 16:3).

March 12: Adar II 1 ends at sunset. Adar II is the last month of the Jewish year and has twenty-nine days.

April 2024 (Jewish Year 5784)						
Sunday	Monday	Tuesday	Wednesday	Thursday	Friday	Saturday
	1 Adar II 21 386 356	2 Adar II 22 387 357	3 Adar II 23 388 358	4 Adar II 24 389 359	5 Adar II 25 390 360	6 Adar II 26 391 361
7 Adar II 27 392 362	8 Adar II 28 393 363	9 Adar II 29 394 364	10 Nisan 1 395 365	11 Nisan 2 396 366	12 Nisan 3 397 367	13 Nisan 4 398 368
14 Nisan 5 399 369	15 Nisan 6 400 370	16 Nisan 7 401 371	17 Nisan 8 402 372	18 Nisan 9 403 373	19 Nisan 10 404 374	20 Nisan 11 405 375
21 Nisan 12 406 376	22 Nisan 13 407 377	23 Nisan 14 408 378	24 Nisan 15 409 379	25 Nisan 16 410 380	26 Nisan 17 411 381	27 Nisan 18 412 382
28 Nisan 19 413 383	29 Nisan 20 414 384	30 Nisan 21 415 385	Nisan is the first month of the Jewish religious calendar and has thirty days.			

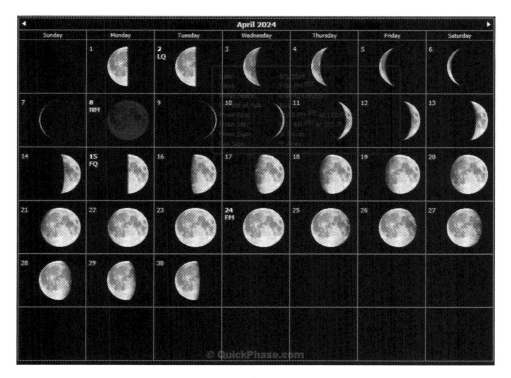

April 2024

April 9: Adar II 29 ends at sunset (6:08 p.m.) and starts Nisan 1.

April 10: Nisan 1 ends at sunset. Nisan is the first month of the Jewish religious calendar and has thirty days.

May 2024 (Jewish Year 5784)						
Sunday	Monday	Tuesday	Wednesday	Thursday	Friday	Saturday
			1 Nisan 22 416 386	**2** Nisan 23 417 387	**3** Nisan 24 418 388	**4** Nisan 25 419 389
5 Nisan 26 420 390	**6** Nisan 27 421 391	**7** Nisan 28 422 392	**8** Nisan 29 423 393	**9** Nisan 30 424 394	**10** Lyyar 1 425 395	**11** Lyyar 2 426 396
12 Lyyar 3 427 397	**13** Lyyar 4 428 398	**14** Lyyar 5 429 399	**15** Lyyar 6 430 400	**16** Lyyar 7 431 401	**17** Lyyar 8 432 402	**18** Lyyar 9 433 403
19 Lyyar 10 434 404	**20** Lyyar 11 435 405	**21** Lyyar 12 436 406	**22** Lyyar 13 437 407	**23** Lyyar 14 438 408	**24** Lyyar 15 439 409	**25** Lyyar 16 440 410
26 Lyyar 17 441 411	**27** Lyyar 18 442 412	**28** Lyyar 19 443 413	**29** Lyyar 20 444 414	**30** Lyyar 21 445 415	**31** Lyyar 22 446 416	

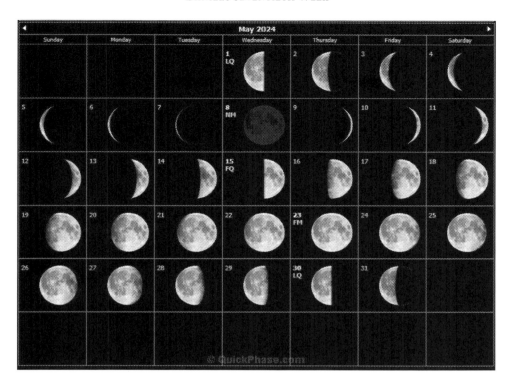

May 2024

June 2024 (Jewish Year 5784)						
Sunday	Monday	Tuesday	Wednesday	Thursday	Friday	Saturday
June 6: Yom Yerushalayim, the fifty-seventh anniversary of Israel reclaiming the Holy City (Jerusalem).					**1** Lyyar 23 447 417	
2 Lyyar 24 448 418	**3** Lyyar 25 449 419	**4** Lyyar 26 450 420	**5** Lyyar 27 451 421	**6** Lyyar 28 452 422	**7** Lyyar 29 453 423	**8** Sivan 1 454 424
9 Sivan 2 455 425	**10** Sivan 3 456 426	**11** Sivan 4 457 427	**12** Sivan 5 458 428	**13** Sivan 6 459 429	**14** Sivan 7 460 430	**15** Sivan 8 461 431
16 Sivan 9 462 432	**17** Sivan 10 463 433	**18** Sivan 11 464 434	**19** Sivan 12 465 435	**20** Sivan 13 466 436	**21** Sivan 14 467 437	**22** Sivan 15 468 438
23 Sivan 16 469 439	**24** Sivan 17 470 440	**25** Sivan 18 471 441	**26** Sivan 19 472 442	**27** Sivan 20 473 443	**28** Sivan 21 474 444	**29** Sivan 22 475 445
30 Sivan 23 476 446						

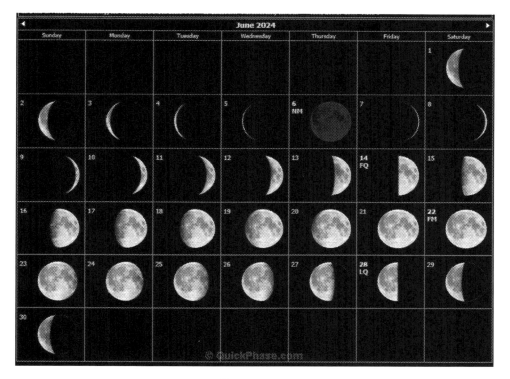

June 2024>

June 7: Lyyar 29 ends at sunset (6:49 p.m.) and starts Sivan 1.

June 8: Sivan 1 ends at sunset. Sivan is the third month of the Jewish calendar and has thirty days.

July 2024 (Jewish Year 5784)						
Sunday	Monday	Tuesday	Wednesday	Thursday	Friday	Saturday
	1 Sivan 24 477 447	2 Sivan 25 478 448	3 Sivan 26 479 449	4 Sivan 27 480 450	5 Sivan 28 481 451	6 Sivan 29 482 452
7 Sivan 30 483 453	8 Tamuz 1 484 454	9 Tamuz 2 485 455	10 Tamuz 3 486 456	11 Tamuz 4 487 457	12 Tamuz 5 488 458	13 Tamuz 6 489 459
14 Tamuz 7 490 460	15 Tamuz 8 491 461	16 Tamuz 9 492 462	17 Tamuz 10 493 463	18 Tamuz 11 494 464	19 Tamuz 12 495 465	20 Tamuz 13 496 466
21 Tamuz 14 497 467	22 Tamuz 15 498 468	23 Tamuz 16 499 469	24 Tamuz 17 500 470	25 Tamuz 18 501 471	26 Tamuz 19 502 472	27 Tamuz 20 503 473
28 Tamuz 21 504 474	29 Tamuz 22 505 475	30 Tamuz 23 506 476	31 Tamuz 24 507 477	*Tamuz 1*: Third vial of God's wrath is poured out.		

Rosh Chodesh Tamuz

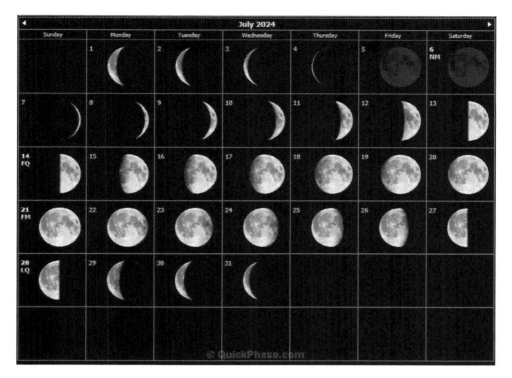

July 2024

July 7: Sivan 30 ends at sunset (6:53 p.m.) and starts Tamuz 1.

Tamuz 1: "And the third angel poured out his vial upon the rivers and fountains of waters; and they became blood" (Rev. 16:4).

July 8: Tamuz 1 ends at sunset. Tamuz is the fourth month of the Jewish calendar and has twenty-nine days.

August 2024 (Jewish Year 5784)						
Sunday	Monday	Tuesday	Wednesday	Thursday	Friday	Saturday
				1 Tamuz 25 **508** **478**	**2** Tamuz 26 **509** **479**	**3** Tamuz 27 **510** **480**
4 Tamuz 28 **511** **482**	**5** Tamuz 29 **512** **483**	**6** Av 1 **513** **484**	**7** Av 2 **514** **484**	**8** Av 3 **515** **485**	**9** Av 4 **516** **486**	**10** Av 5 **517** **487**
11 Av 6 **518** **488**	**12** Av 7 **519** **489**	**13** Av 8 **520** **490**	**14** Av 9 **521** **491**	**15** Av 10 **522** **492**	**16** Av 11 **523** **493**	**17** Av 12 **524** **494**
18 Av 13 **525** **495**	**19** Av 14 **526** **496**	**20** Av 15 **527** **497**	**21** Av 16 **528** **498**	**22** Av 17 **529** **499**	**23** Av 18 **530** **500**	**24** Av 19 **531** **501**
25 Av 20 **532** **502**	**26** Av 21 **533** **503**	**27** Av 22 **534** **504**	**28** Av 23 **535** **505**	**29** Av 24 **536** **506**	**30** Av 25 **537** **507**	**31** Av 26 **538** **508**

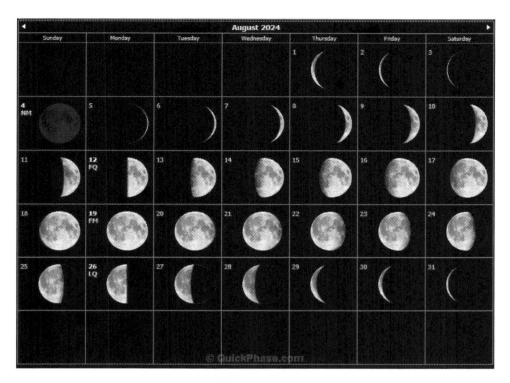

August 2024

September 2024 (Jewish Year 5784)						
Sunday	Monday	Tuesday	Wednesday	Thursday	Friday	Saturday
1 Av 27 539 509	2 Av 28 540 510	3 Av 29 541 511	4 Av 30 542 512	5 Elul 1 543 513	6 Elul 2 544 514	7 Elul 3 545 515
8 Elul 4 546 516	9 Elul 5 547 517	10 Elul 6 548 518	11 Elul 7 549 519	12 Elul 8 550 520	13 Elul 9 551 521	14 Elul 10 552 522
15 Elul 11 553 523	16 Elul 12 554 524	17 Elul 13 555 525	18 Elul 14 556 526	19 Elul 15 557 527	20 Elul 16 558 528	21 Elul 17 559 529
22 Elul 18 560 530	23 Elul 19 561 531	24 Elul 20 562 532	25 Elul 21 563 533	26 Elul 22 564 534	27 Elul 23 565 535	28 Elul 24 566 536
29 Elul 25 567 537	30 Elul 26 568 538					

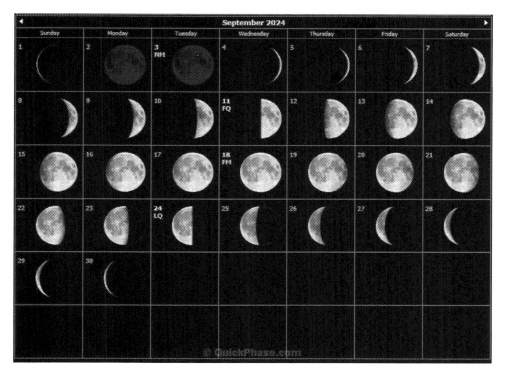

September 2024

October 2024 (Jewish Year 5784/5785)						
Sunday	Monday	Tuesday	Wednesday	Thursday	Friday	Saturday
		1 Elul 27 569 539	2 Elul 28 570 540	3 Elul 29 571 541	4 Tishri 1 572 542	5 Tishri 2 573 543
6 Tishri 3 574 544	7 Tishri 4 575 545	8 Tishri 5 576 546	9 Tishri 6 577 547	10 Tishri 7 578 548	11 Tishri 8 579 549	12 Tishri 9 580 550
13 Tishri 10 581 551	14 Tishri 11 582 552	15 Tishri 12 583 553	16 Tishri 13 584 554	17 Tishri 14 585 555	18 Tishri 15 586 556	19 Tishri 16 587 557
20 Tishri 17 588 558	21 Tishri 18 589 559	22 Tishri 19 590 560	23 Tishri 20 591 561	24 Tishri 21 592 562	25 Tishri 22 593 563	26 Tishri 23 594 564
27 Tishri 24 595 565	28 Tishri 25 596 566	29 Tishri 26 597 567	30 Tishri 27 598 568	31 Tishri 28 599 569		

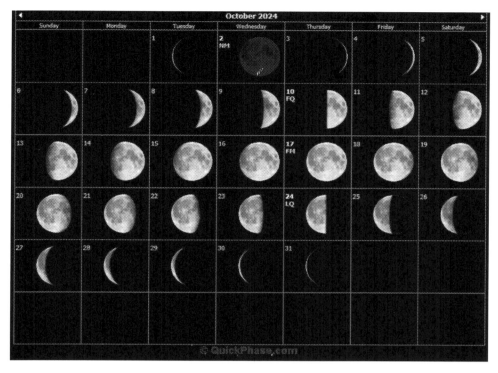

October 2024

November 2024 (Jewish Year 5785)						
Sunday	Monday	Tuesday	Wednesday	Thursday	Friday	Saturday
					1 Tishri 29 600 570	**2** Tishri 30 601 571
3 Cheshvan 1 602 572	**4** Cheshvan 2 603 573	**5** Cheshvan 3 604 574	**6** Cheshvan 4 605 575	**7** Cheshvan 5 606 576	**8** Cheshvan 6 607 577	**9** Cheshvan 7 608 578
10 Cheshvan 8 609 579	**11** Cheshvan 9 610 580	**12** Cheshvan 10 611 581	**13** Cheshvan 11 612 582	**14** Cheshvan 12 613 583	**15** Cheshvan 13 614 584	**16** Cheshvan 14 615 585
17 Cheshvan 15 616 586	**18** Cheshvan 16 617 587	**19** Cheshvan 17 618 588	**20** Cheshvan 18 619 589	**21** Cheshvan 19 620 590	**22** Cheshvan 20 621 591	**23** Cheshvan 21 622 592
24 Cheshvan 22 623 593	**25** Cheshvan 23 624 594	**26** Cheshvan 24 625 595	**27** Cheshvan 25 626 596	**28** Cheshvan 26 627 597	**29** Cheshvan 27 628 598	**30** Cheshvan 28 629 599

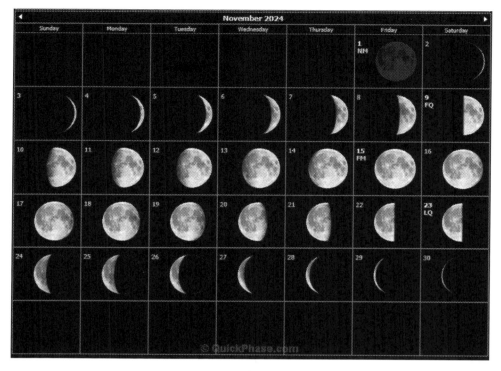

November 2024

November 2: Tishri 30 ends at sunset (4:49 p.m.) and starts Cheshvan 1.

Cheshvan 1: "And the fourth angel poured out his vial upon the sun; and power was given unto him to scorch men with fire. And men were scorched with great heat, and blasphemed the name of God, which hath power over these plagues: and they repented not to give him glory" (Rev. 16:8–9).

November 3: Cheshvan 1 ends at sunset.

December 2024 (Jewish Year 5785)						
Sunday	Monday	Tuesday	Wednesday	Thursday	Friday	Saturday
1 Cheshvan 29 630 600	2 Cheshvan 30 631 601	3 Kislev 1 632 602	4 Kislev 2 633 603	5 Kislev 3 634 604	6 Kislev 4 635 605	7 Kislev 5 636 606
8 Kislev 6 637 607	9 Kislev 7 638 608	10 Kislev 8 639 609	11 Kislev 9 640 610	12 Kislev 10 641 611	13 Kislev 11 642 612	14 Kislev 12 643 613
15 Kislev 13 644 614	16 Kislev 14 645 615	17 Kislev 15 646 616	18 Kislev 16 647 617	19 Kislev 17 648 618	20 Kislev 18 649 619	21 Kislev 19 650 620
22 Kislev 20 651 621	23 Kislev 21 652 622	24 Kislev 22 653 623	25 Kislev 23 654 624	26 Kislev 24 655 625	27 Kislev 25 656 626	28 Kislev 26 657 627
29 Kislev 27 658 628	30 Kislev 28 659 629	31 Kislev 29 660 630				

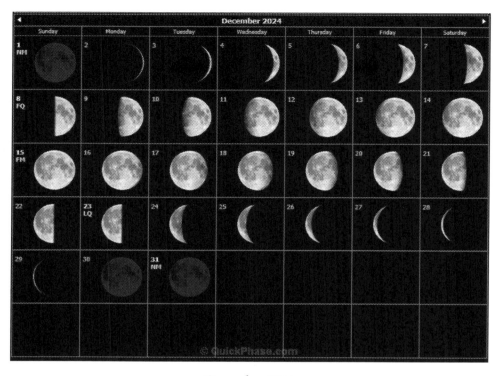

December 2024

January 2025 (Jewish Year 5785)						
Sunday	Monday	Tuesday	Wednesday	Thursday	Friday	Saturday
			1 Tevet 1 661 631	2 Tevet 2 662 632	3 Tevet 3 663 633	4 Tevet 4 664 634
5 Tevet 5 665 635	6 Tevet 6 666 636	7 Tevet 7 667 637	8 Tevet 8 668 638	9 Tevet 9 669 639	10 Tevet 10 670 640	11 Tevet 11 671 641
12 Tevet 12 672 642	13 Tevet 13 673 643	14 Tevet 14 674 644	15 Tevet 15 675 645	16 Tevet 16 676 646	17 Tevet 17 677 647	18 Tevet 18 678 648
19 Tevet 19 679 649	20 Tevet 20 680 650	21 Tevet 21 681 651	22 Tevet 22 682 652	23 Tevet 23 683 653	24 Tevet 24 684 654	25 Tevet 25 685 655
26 Tevet 26 686 656	27 Tevet 27 687 657	28 Tevet 28 688 658	29 Tevet 29 689 659	30 Sh'vat 1 690 660	31 Sh'vat 2 691 661	

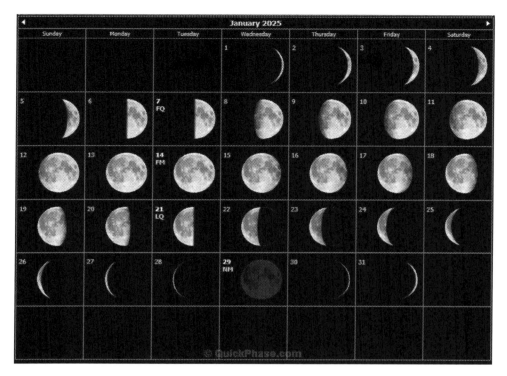

January 2025

January 1: Tevet 1 ends at sunset. Tevet is the tenth month of the Jewish calendar and has twenty-nine days.

January 29: Tevet 29 ends at sunset (4:34 p.m.) and starts Sh'vat 1.

January 30: Sh'vat 1 ends at sunset. Sh'vat is the eleventh month of the Jewish calendar and has thirty days.

February 2025 (Jewish Year 5785)						
Sunday	Monday	Tuesday	Wednesday	Thursday	Friday	Saturday
						1 Sh'vat 3 **692** **662**
2 Sh'vat 4 **693** **663**	**3** Sh'vat 5 **694** **664**	**4** Sh'vat 6 **695** **665**	**5** Sh'vat 7 **696** **666**	**6** Sh'vat 8 **697** **667**	**7** Sh'vat 9 **698** **668**	**8** Sh'vat 10 **699** **669**
9 Sh'vat 11 **700** **670**	**10** Sh'vat 12 **701** **671**	**11** Sh'vat 13 **702** **672**	**12** Sh'vat 14 **703** **673**	**13** Sh'vat 15 **704** **674**	**14** Sh'vat 16 **705** **675**	**15** Sh'vat 17 **706** **676**
16 Sh'vat 18 **707** **677**	**17** Sh'vat 19 **708** **678**	**18** Sh'vat 20 **709** **679**	**19** Sh'vat 21 **710** **680**	**20** Sh'vat 22 **711** **681**	**21** Sh'vat 23 **712** **682**	**22** Sh'vat 24 **713** **683**
23 Sh'vat 25 **714** **684**	**24** Sh'vat 26 **715** **685**	**25** Sh'vat 27 **716** **686**	**26** Sh'vat 28 **717** **687**	**27** Sh'vat 29 **718** **688**	**28** Sh'vat 30 **719** **689**	

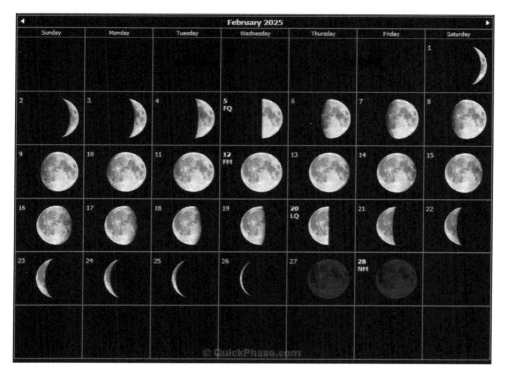

February 2025

February 28: Sh'vat 30 ends at sunset (5:38 p.m.) and starts Adar 1.

March 2025 (Jewish Year 5785)						
Sunday	Monday	Tuesday	Wednesday	Thursday	Friday	Saturday
						1 Adar 1 **720** **690**
2 Adar 2 **721** **691**	**3** Adar 3 **722** **692**	**4** Adar 4 **723** **693**	**5** Adar 5 **724** **694**	**6** Adar 6 **725** **695**	**7** Adar 7 **726** **696**	**8** Adar 8 **727** **697**
9 Adar 9 **728** **698**	**10** Adar 10 **729** **699**	**11** Adar 11 **730** **700**	**12** Adar 12 **731** **701**	**13** Adar 13 **732** **702**	**14** Adar 14 **733** **703**	**15** Adar 15 **734** **704**
16 Adar 16 **735** **705**	**17** Adar 17 **736** **706**	**18** Adar 18 **737** **707**	**19** Adar 19 **738** **708**	**20** Adar 20 **739** **709**	**21** Adar 21 **740** **710**	**22** Adar 22 **741** **711**
23 Adar 23 **742** **712**	**24** Adar 24 **743** **713**	**25** Adar 25 **744** **714**	**26** Adar 26 **745** **715**	**27** Adar 27 **746** **716**	**28** Adar 28 **747** **717**	**29** Adar 29 **748** **718**
30 Nisan 1 **749** **719**	**31** Nisan 2 **750** **720**	Adar is the twelfth month of the Jewish year and has twenty-nine days.				

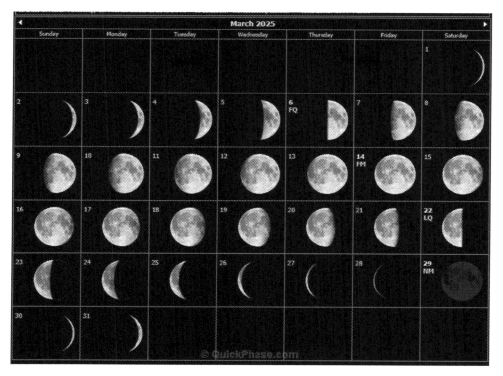

March 2025

Adar 1: "And the fifth angel poured out his vial upon the seat of the beast; and his kingdom was full of darkness; and they gnawed their tongues for pain, And blasphemed the God of heaven because of their pains and their sores, and repented not of their deeds" (Rev. 16:10–11).

March 1: Adar 1 ends at sunset.

April 2025 (Jewish Year 5785)						
Sunday	Monday	Tuesday	Wednesday	Thursday	Friday	Saturday
Nisan is the first month of the Jewish year and has thirty days.		1 Nisan 3 751 721	2 Nisan 4 752 722	3 Nisan 5 753 723	4 Nisan 6 754 724	5 Nisan 7 755 725
6 Nisan 8 756 726	7 Nisan 9 757 727	8 Nisan 10 758 728	9 Nisan 11 759 729	10 Nisan 12 760 730	11 Nisan 13 761 731	12 Nisan 14 762 732
13 Nisan 15 763 733	14 Nisan 16 764 734	15 Nisan 17 765 735	16 Nisan 18 766 736	17 Nisan 19 767 737	18 Nisan 20 768 738	19 Nisan 21 769 739
20 Nisan 22 770 740	21 Nisan 23 771 741	22 Nisan 24 772 742	23 Nisan 25 773 743	24 Nisan 26 774 744	25 Nisan 27 775 745	26 Nisan 28 776 746
27 Nisan 29 777 747	28 Nisan 30 778 748	29 Lyyar 1 779 749	30 Lyyar 2 780 750	Lyyar is the second month of the Jewish calendar and has twenty-nine days.		

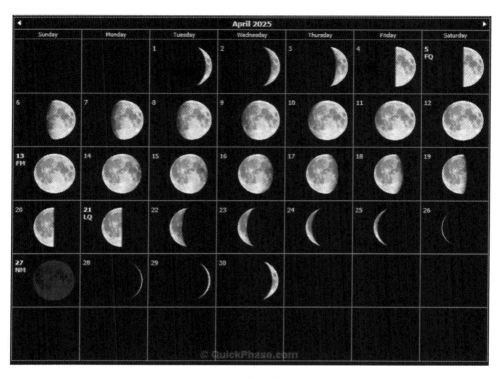

April 2025

May 2025 (Jewish Year 5785)						
Sunday	Monday	Tuesday	Wednesday	Thursday	Friday	Saturday
May 26: Yom Yerushalayim, the fifty-eighth anniversary of Israel reclaiming the Holy City (Jerusalem).				1 Lyyar 3 781 751	2 Lyyar 4 782 752	3 Lyyar 5 783 753
4 Lyyar 6 784 754	5 Lyyar 7 785 755	6 Lyyar 8 786 756	7 Lyyar 9 787 757	8 Lyyar 10 788 758	9 Lyyar 11 789 759	10 Lyyar 12 790 760
11 Lyyar 13 791 761	12 Lyyar 14 792 762	13 Lyyar 15 793 763	14 Lyyar 16 794 764	15 Lyyar 17 795 765	16 Lyyar 18 796 766	17 Lyyar 19 797 767
18 Lyyar 20 798 768	19 Lyyar 21 799 769	20 Lyyar 22 800 770	21 Lyyar 23 801 771	22 Lyyar 24 802 772	23 Lyyar 25 803 773	17 Lyyar 26 804 774
25 Lyyar 27 805 775	26 Lyyar 28 806 776	27 Lyyar 29 807 777	28 Sivan 1 808 778	29 Sivan 2 809 779	30 Sivan 3 810 780	31 Sivan 4 811 781

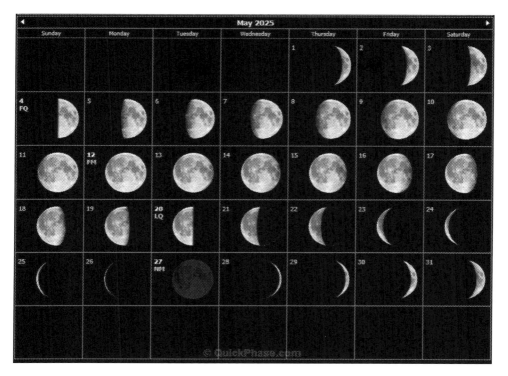

May 2025

April 27: Lyyar 29 end at sunset (6:42 p.m.) and starts Sivan 1.

April 28: Sivan 1 ends at sunset. Sivan is the third month of the Jewish year and has thirty days.

June 2025 (Jewish Year 5785)						
Sunday	Monday	Tuesday	Wednesday	Thursday	Friday	Saturday
1 Sivan 5 812 782	2 Sivan 6 813 783	3 Sivan 7 814 784	4 Sivan 8 815 785	5 Sivan 9 816 786	6 Sivan 10 817 787	7 Sivan 11 818 788
8 Sivan 12 819 789	9 Sivan 13 820 790	10 Sivan 14 821 791	11 Sivan 15 822 792	12 Sivan 16 823 793	13 Sivan 17 824 794	14 Sivan 18 825 795
15 Sivan 19 826 796	16 Sivan 20 827 797	17 Sivan 21 828 798	18 Sivan 22 829 799	19 Sivan 23 830 800	20 Sivan 24 831 801	21 Sivan 25 832 802
22 Sivan 26 833 803	23 Sivan 27 834 804	24 Sivan 28 835 805	25 Sivan 29 836 806	26 Sivan 30 837 807	27 Tamuz 1 838 808	28 Tamuz 2 839 809
29 Tamuz 3 840 810	30 Tamuz 4 841 811					

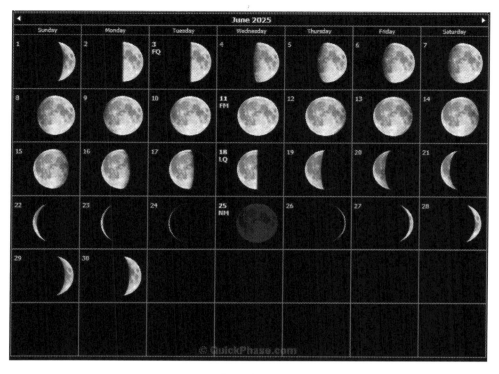

June 2025

July 2025 (Jewish Year 5785)						
Sunday	Monday	Tuesday	Wednesday	Thursday	Friday	Saturday
		1 Tamuz 5 842 812	2 Tamuz 6 843 813	3 Tamuz 7 844 814	4 Tamuz 8 845 815	5 Tamuz 9 846 816
6 Tamuz 10 847 817	7 Tamuz 11 848 818	8 Tamuz 12 849 819	9 Tamuz 13 850 820	10 Tamuz 14 851 821	11 Tamuz 15 852 822	12 Tamuz 16 853 823
13 Tamuz 17 854 824	14 Tamuz 18 855 825	15 Tamuz 19 856 826	16 Tamuz 20 857 827	17 Tamuz 21 858 828	18 Tamuz 22 859 829	19 Tamuz 23 860 830
20 Tamuz 24 861 831	21 Tamuz 25 862 832	22 Tamuz 26 863 833	23 Tamuz 27 864 834	24 Tamuz 28 865 835	25 Tamuz 29 866 836	26 Av 1 867 837
27 Av 2 868 838	28 Av 3 869 839	29 Av 4 870 840	30 Av 5 871 841	31 Av 6 872 842		

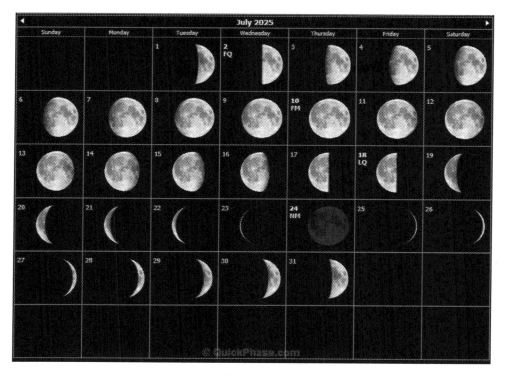

July 2025

July 25: Tamuz 29 ends at sunset (6:46 p.m.) and starts Av 1.

August 2025 (Jewish Year 5785)						
Sunday	Monday	Tuesday	Wednesday	Thursday	Friday	Saturday
					1 Av 7 873 843	**2** Av 8 874 844
3 Av 9 875 845	**4** Av 10 876 846	**5** Av 11 877 847	**6** Av 12 878 848	**7** Av 13 879 849	**8** Av 14 880 850	**9** Av 15 881 851
10 Av 16 882 852	**11** Av 17 883 853	**12** Av 18 884 854	**13** Av 19 885 855	**14** Av 20 886 856	**15** Av 21 887 857	**16** Av 22 888 858
17 Av 23 889 859	**18** Av 24 890 860	**19** Av 25 891 861	**20** Av 26 892 862	**21** Av 27 893 863	**22** Av 28 894 864	**23** Av 29 895 865
24 Av 30 896 866	**25** Elul 1 897 867	**26** Elul 2 898 868	**27** Elul 3 899 869	**28** Elul 4 900 870	**29** Elul 5 901 871	**30** Elul 6 902 872
31 Elul 7 903 873						

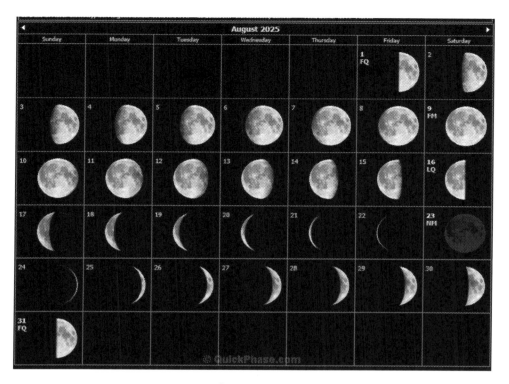

August 2025

September 2025 (Jewish Year 5785/5786)						
Sunday	Monday	Tuesday	Wednesday	Thursday	Friday	Saturday
	1 Elul 8 904 874	2 Elul 9 905 875	3 Elul 10 906 876	4 Elul 11 907 877	5 Elul 12 908 878	6 Elul 13 909 879
7 Elul 14 910 880	8 Elul 15 911 881	9 Elul 16 912 882	10 Elul 17 913 883	11 Elul 18 914 884	12 Elul 19 915 885	13 Elul 20 916 886
14 Elul 21 917 887	15 Elul 22 918 888	16 Elul 23 919 889	17 Elul 24 920 890	18 Elul 25 921 891	19 Elul 26 922 892	20 Elul 27 923 893
21 Elul 28 924 894	22 Elul 29 925 895	23 Tishri 1 926 896	24 Tishri 2 927 897	25 Tishri 3 928 898	26 Tishri 4 929 899	27 Tishri 5 930 900
28 Tishri 6 931 901	29 Tishri 7 932 902	30 Tishri 8 933 903	*September 22*: Elul 29 ends at sunset (5:38 p.m.) and starts Tishri 1.			

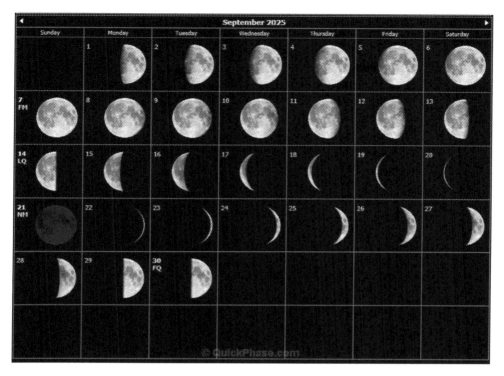

September 2025

October 2025 (Jewish Year 5786)						
Sunday	Monday	Tuesday	Wednesday	Thursday	Friday	Saturday
			1 Tishri 9 934 904	**2** Tishri 10 935 905	**3** Tishri 11 936 906	**4** Tishri 12 937 907
5 Tishri 13 938 908	**6** Tishri 14 939 909	**7** Tishri 15 940 910	**8** Tishri 16 941 911	**9** Tishri 17 942 912	**10** Tishri 18 943 913	**11** Tishri 19 944 914
12 Tishri 20 945 915	**13** Tishri 21 946 916	**14** Tishri 22 947 917	**15** Tishri 23 948 918	**16** Tishri 24 949 919	**17** Tishri 25 950 920	**18** Tishri 26 951 921
19 Tishri 27 952 922	**20** Tishri 28 953 923	**21** Tishri 29 954 924	**22** Tishri 30 955 925	**23** Cheshvan 1 956 926	**24** Cheshvan 2 957 927	**25** Cheshvan 3 958 928
26 Cheshvan 4 959 929	**27** Cheshvan 5 960 930	**28** Cheshvan 6 961 931	**29** Cheshvan 7 962 932	**30** Cheshvan 8 963 933	**31** Cheshvan 9 964 934	

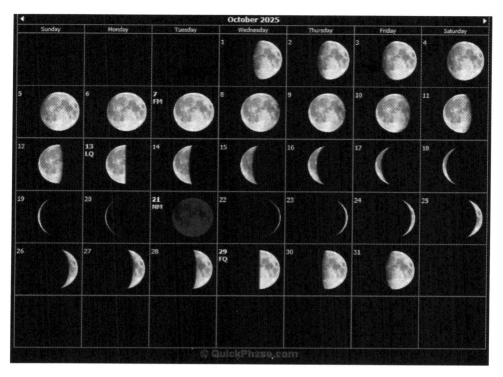

October 2025

November 2025 (Jewish Year 5786)						
Sunday	Monday	Tuesday	Wednesday	Thursday	Friday	Saturday
						1 Cheshvan 10 *965* *935*
2 Cheshvan 11 *966* *936*	**3** Cheshvan 12 *967* *937*	**4** Cheshvan 13 *968* *938*	**5** Cheshvan 14 *969* *939*	**6** Cheshvan 15 *970* *940*	**7** Cheshvan 16 *971* *941*	**8** Cheshvan 17 *972* *942*
9 Cheshvan 18 *973* *943*	**10** Cheshvan 19 *974* *944*	**11** Cheshvan 20 *975* *945*	**12** Cheshvan 21 *976* *946*	**13** Cheshvan 22 *977* *947*	**14** Cheshvan 23 *978* *948*	**15** Cheshvan 24 *979* *949*
16 Cheshvan 25 *980* *950*	**17** Cheshvan 26 *981* *951*	**18** Cheshvan 27 *982* *952*	**19** Cheshvan 28 *983* *953*	**20** Cheshvan 29 *984* *954*	**21** Cheshvan 30 *985* *955*	**22** Kislev 1 *986* *956*
23 Kislev 2 *987* *957*	**24** Kislev 3 *988* *958*	**25** Kislev 4 *989* *959*	**26** Kislev 5 *990* *960*	**27** Kislev 6 *991* *961*	**28** Kislev 7 *992* *962*	**29** Kislev 8 *993* *963*
30 Kislev 9 *994* *964*	Cheshvan 30 ends at sunset (4:37 p.m.) and starts Kislev 1.					

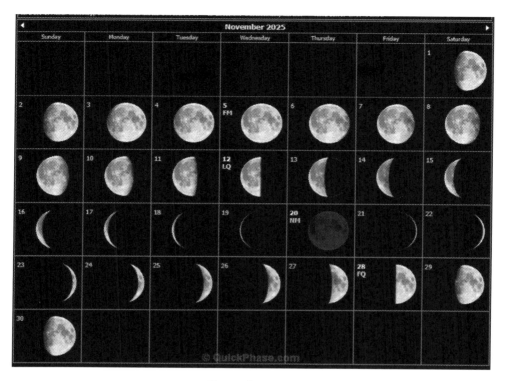

November 2025

November 21: Cheshvan 30 ends at sunset (4:37 p.m.) and starts Kislev 1.

December 2025 (Jewish Year 5786)						
Sunday	Monday	Tuesday	Wednesday	Thursday	Friday	Saturday
	1 Kislev 10 995 965	2 Kislev 11 996 966	3 Kislev 12 997 967	4 Kislev 13 998 968	5 Kislev 14 999 969	6 Kislev 15 1000 970
7 Kislev 16 1001 971	8 Kislev 17 1002 972	9 Kislev 18 1003 973	10 Kislev 19 1004 974	11 Kislev 20 1005 975	12 Kislev 21 1006 976	13 Kislev 22 1007 977
14 Kislev 23 1008 978	15 Kislev 24 1009 979	16 Kislev 25 1010 980	17 Kislev 26 1011 981	18 Kislev 27 1012 982	19 Kislev 28 1013 983	20 Kislev 29 1014 984
21 Kislev 30 1015 985	22 Tevet 1 1016 986	23 Tevet 2 1017 987	24 Tevet 3 1018 988	25 Tevet 4 1019 989	26 Tevet 5 1020 990	27 Tevet 6 1021 991
28 Tevet 7 1022 992	29 Tevet 8 1023 993	30 Tevet 9 1024 994	31 Tevet 10 1025 995	Tevet is the tenth month of the Jewish religious calendar and has twenty-nine days.		

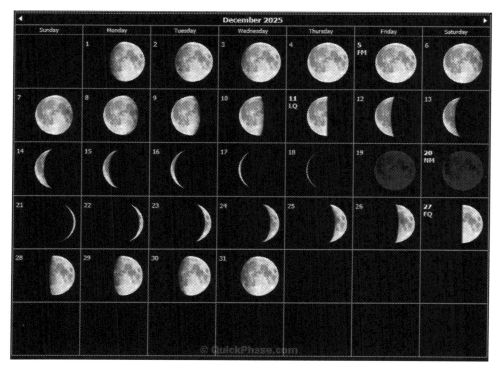

December 2025

December 21: Kislev 30 ends at sunset (4:39 p.m.) and starts Tevet 1.

January 2026 (Jewish Year 5786)						
Sunday	Monday	Tuesday	Wednesday	Thursday	Friday	Saturday
				1 Tevet 11 **1026** 996	**2** Tevet 12 **1027** 997	**3** Tevet 13 **1028** 998
4 Tevet 14 **1029** 999	**5** Tevet 15 **1030** 1000	**6** Tevet 16 **1031** 1001	**7** Tevet 17 **1032** 1002	**8** Tevet 18 **1033** 1003	**9** Tevet 19 **1034** 1004	**10** Tevet 20 **1035** 1005
11 Tevet 21 **1036** 1006	**12** Tevet 22 **1037** 1007	**13** Tevet 23 **1038** 1008	**14** Tevet 24 **1039** 1009	**15** Tevet 25 **1040** 1010	**16** Tevet 26 **1041** 1011	**17** Tevet 27 **1042** 1012
18 Tevet 28 **1043** 1013	**19** Tevet 29 **1044** 1014	**20** Sh'vat 1 **1045** 1015	**21** Sh'vat 2 **1046** 1016	**22** Sh'vat 3 **1047** 1017	**23** Sh'vat 4 **1048** 1018	**24** Sh'vat 5 **1049** 1019
25 Sh'vat 6 **1050** 1020	**26** Sh'vat 7 **1051** 1021	**27** Sh'vat 8 **1052** 1022	**28** Sh'vat 9 **1053** 1023	**29** Sh'vat 10 **1054** 1024	**30** Sh'vat 11 **1055** 1025	**31** Sh'vat 12 **1056** 1026

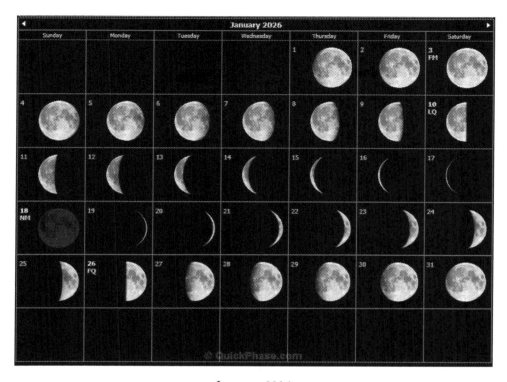

January 2026

January 19: Tevet 29 ends at sunset (5:01 p.m.) and starts Sh'vat 1.

Sh'vat 1: "And the sixth angel poured out his vial upon the great river Euphrates; and the water thereof was dried up, that the way of the kings of the east might be prepared. And I saw three unclean spirits like frogs *come* out of the mouth of the dragon, and out of the mouth of the beast, and out of the mouth of the false prophet. For they are the spirits of devils, working miracles, *which* go forth unto the kings of the earth and of the whole world, to gather them to the battle of that great day of God Almighty. Behold, I come as a thief. Blessed *is* he that watcheth, and keepeth his garments, lest he walk naked, and they see his shame. And he gathered them together into a place called in the Hebrew tongue Armageddon" (Rev. 16:12–16).

February 2026 (Jewish Year 5786)						
Sunday	Monday	Tuesday	Wednesday	Thursday	Friday	Saturday
1 Sh'vat 13 1057 1027	2 Sh'vat 14 1058 1028	3 Sh'vat 15 1059 1029	4 Sh'vat 16 1060 1030	5 Sh'vat 17 1061 1031	6 Sh'vat 18 1062 1032	7 Sh'vat 19 1063 1033
8 Sh'vat 20 1064 1034	9 Sh'vat 21 1065 1035	10 Sh'vat 22 1066 1036	11 Sh'vat 23 1067 1037	12 Sh'vat 24 1068 1038	13 Sh'vat 25 1069 1039	14 Sh'vat 26 1070 1040
15 Sh'vat 27 1071 1041	16 Sh'vat 28 1072 1042	17 Sh'vat 29 1073 1043	18 Sh'vat 30 1074 1044	19 Adar 1 1075 1045	20 Adar 2 1076 1046	21 Adar 3 1077 1047
22 Adar 4 1078 1048	23 Adar 5 1079 1049	24 Adar 6 1080 1050	25 Adar 7 1081 1051	26 Adar 8 1082 1052	27 Adar 9 1083 1053	28 Adar 10 1084 1054

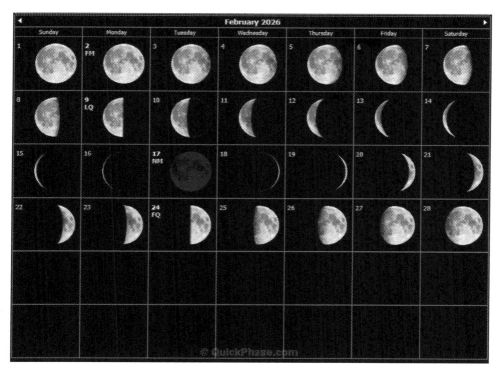

February 2026

February 18: Sh'vat 30 ends at sunset (5:29 p.m.) and starts Adar 1.

March 2026 (Jewish Year 5786)						
Sunday	**Monday**	**Tuesday**	**Wednesday**	**Thursday**	**Friday**	**Saturday**
1 Adar 11 1085 1055	2 Adar 12 1086 1056	3 Adar 13 1087 1057	4 Adar 14 1088 1058	5 Adar 15 1089 1059	6 Adar 16 1090 1060	7 Adar 17 1091 1061
8 Adar 18 1092 1062	9 Adar 19 1093 1063	10 Adar 20 1094 1064	11 Adar 21 1095 1065	12 Adar 22 1096 1066	13 Adar 23 1097 1067	14 Adar 24 1098 1068
15 Adar 25 1099 1069	16 Adar 26 1000 1070	17 Adar 27 1001 1071	18 Adar 28 1102 1072	19 Adar 29 1103 1073	20 Nisan 1 1104 1074	21 Nisan 2 1105 1075
22 Nisan 3 1106 1076	23 Nisan 4 1107 1077	24 Nisan 5 1108 1078	25 Nisan 6 1109 1079	26 Nisan 7 1110 1080	27 Nisan 8 1111 1081	28 Nisan 9 1112 1082
29 Nisan 10 1113 1083	30 Nisan 11 1114 1084	31 Nisan 12 1115 1085	*March 19*: Adar 29 ends at sunset (5:52 p.m.) and starts Nisan 1.			

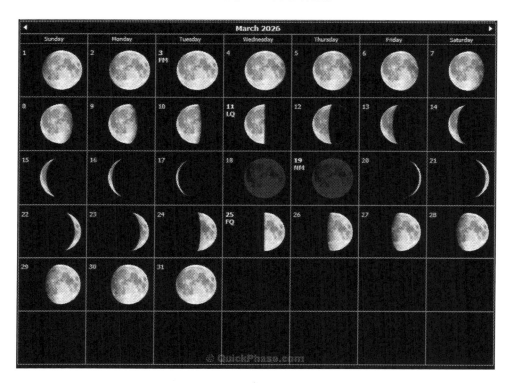

March 2026

March 19: Adar 29 ends at sunset (5:52 p.m.) and starts Nisan 1.

March 20: Nisan 1 ends at sunset.

April 2026 (Jewish Year 5786)						
Sunday	Monday	Tuesday	Wednesday	Thursday	Friday	Saturday
			1 Nisan 13 **1116** **1086**	**2** Nisan 14 **1117** **1087**	**3** Nisan 15 **1118** **1088**	**4** Nisan 16 **1119** **1089**
5 Nisan 17 **1120** **1090**	**6** Nisan 18 **1121** **1091**	**7** Nisan 19 **1122** **1092**	**8** Nisan 20 **1123** **1093**	**9** Nisan 21 **1124** **1094**	**10** Nisan 22 **1125** **1095**	**11** Nisan 23 **1126** **1096**
12 Nisan 24 **1127** **1097**	**13** Nisan 25 **1128** **1098**	**14** Nisan 26 **1129** **1099**	**15** Nisan 27 **1130** **1100**	**16** Nisan 28 **1131** **1101**	**17** Nisan 29 **1132** **1102**	**18** Nisan 30 **1133** **1103**
19 Lyyar 1 **1134** **1104**	**20** Lyyar 2 **1135** **1105**	**21** Lyyar 3 **1136** **1106**	**22** Lyyar 4 **1137** **1107**	**23** Lyyar 5 **1138** **1108**	**24** Lyyar 6 **1139** **1109**	**25** Lyyar 7 **1140** **1110**
26 Lyyar 8 **1141** **1111**	**27** 90 Lyyar **1142** **1112**	**28** Lyyar 10 **1143** **1113**	**29** Lyyar 11 **1144** **1114**	**30** Lyyar 12 **1145** **1115**		

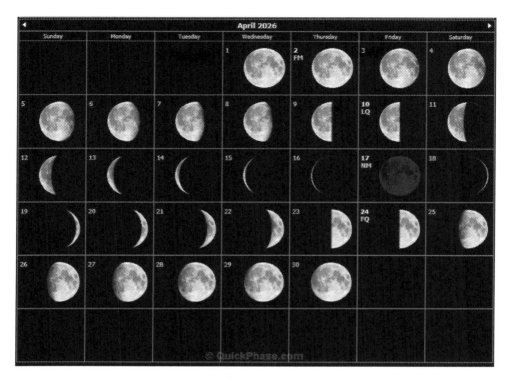

April 2026

April 18: Nisan 30 ends at sunset (6:14 p.m.) and starts Lyyar 1.

May 2026 (Jewish Year 5786)						
Sunday	Monday	Tuesday	Wednesday	Thursday	Friday	Saturday
May 16: Yom Yerushalayim, the fifty-ninth anniversary of Israel reclaiming the Holy City (Jerusalem). *Sivan 1*: An angel pours out the seventh bowl of the wrath of God.					**1** Lyyar 13 **1146** **1116**	**2** Lyyar 14 **1147** **1117**
3 Lyyar 15 **1148** **1118**	**4** Lyyar 16 **1149** **1119**	**5** Lyyar 17 **1150** **1120**	**6** Lyyar 18 **1151** **1121**	**7** Lyyar 19 **1152** **1122**	**8** Lyyar 20 **1153** **1123**	**9** Lyyar 21 **1154** **1124**
10 Lyyar 22 **1155** **1125**	**11** Lyyar 23 **1156** **1126**	**12** Lyyar 24 **1157** **1127**	**13** Lyyar 25 **1158** **1128**	**14** Lyyar 26 **1159** **1129**	**15** Lyyar 27 **1160** **1130**	**16** Lyyar 28 **1161** **1131**
17 Lyyar 29 **1162** **1132**	**18** Sivan 1 **1163** **1133**	**19** Sivan 2 **1164** **1134**	**20** Sivan 3 **1165** **1135**	**21** Sivan 4 **1166** **1136**	**22** Sivan 5 **1167** **1137**	**23** Sivan 6 **1168** **1138**
24 Sivan 7 **1169** **1139**	**25** Sivan 8 **1170** **1140**	**26** Sivan 9 **1171** **1141**	**27** Sivan 10 **1172** **1142**	**28** Sivan 11 **1173** **1143**	**29** Sivan 12 **1174** **1144**	**30** Sivan 13 **1175** **1145**
31 Sivan 14 **1176** **1146**	*Sivan 1*: Every island and mountain is destroyed. A hailstorm occurs, the hail being twelve to twenty gallons of water in size. A talent is between one hundred and two hundred pounds.					

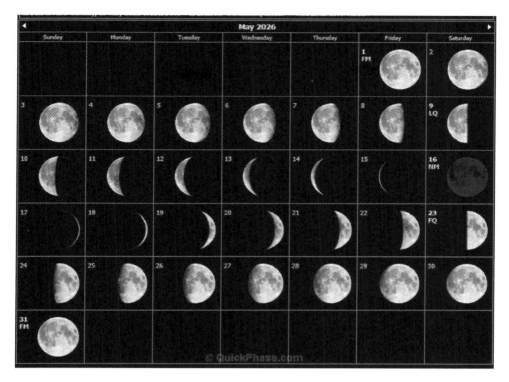

May 2026

May 17: Lyyar 29 ends at sunset (6:35 p.m.) and starts Sivan 1.

Sivan 1: "And the seventh angel poured out his vial into the air; and there came a great voice out of the temple of heaven, from the throne, saying, It is done. And there were voices, and thunders, and lightnings; and there was a great earthquake, such as was not since men were upon the earth, so mighty an earthquake, *and* so great. And the great city was divided into three parts, and the cities of the nations fell: and great Babylon came in remembrance before God, to give unto her the cup of the wine of the fierceness of his wrath. And every island fled away, and the mountains were not found. And there fell upon men a great hail out of heaven, *every stone* about the weight of a talent: and men blasphemed God because of the plague of the hail; for the plague thereof was exceeding great" (Rev. 16:17–21).

June 2026 (Jewish Year 5786)						
Sunday	Monday	Tuesday	Wednesday	Thursday	Friday	Saturday
	1 Sivan 15 1177 1147	2 Sivan 16 1178 1148	3 Sivan 17 1179 1149	4 Sivan 18 1180 1150	5 Sivan 19 1181 1151	6 Sivan 20 1182 1152
7 Sivan 21 1183 1153	8 Sivan 22 1184 1154	9 Sivan 23 1185 1155	10 Sivan 24 1186 1156	11 Sivan 25 1187 1157	12 Sivan 26 1188 1158	13 Sivan 27 1189 1159
14 Sivan 28 1190 1160	15 Sivan 29 1191 1161	16 Sivan 30 1192 1162	17 Tamuz 1 1193 1163	18 Tamuz 2 1194 1164	19 Tamuz 3 1195 1165	20 Tamuz 4 1196 1166
21 Tamuz 5 1197 1167	22 Tamuz 6 1198 1168	23 Tamuz 7 1199 1169	24 Tamuz 8 1200 1170	25 Tamuz 9 1201 1171	26 Tamuz 10 1202 1172	27 Tamuz 11 1203 1173
28 Tamuz 12 1204 1174	29 Tamuz 13 1205 1175	30 Tamuz 14 1206 1176	*June 16*: Sivan 30 ends at sunset (6:52 p.m.) and starts Tamuz 1. Tamuz is the fourth month of the Jewish calendar and has twenty-nine days.			

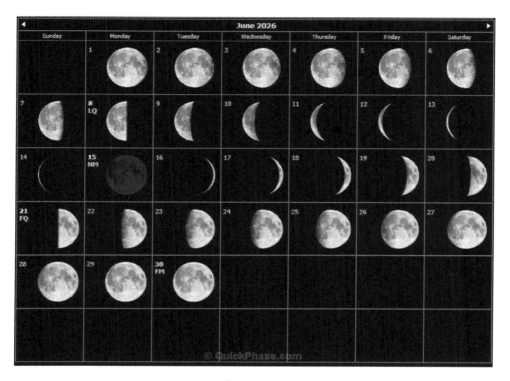

June 2026

July 2026 (Jewish Year 5786)						
Sunday	Monday	Tuesday	Wednesday	Thursday	Friday	Saturday
			1 Tamuz 15 1207 1177	**2** Tamuz 16 1208 1178	**3** Tamuz 17 1209 1179	**4** Tamuz 18 1210 1180
5 Tamuz 19 1211 1181	**6** Tamuz 20 1212 1182	**7** Tamuz 21 1213 1183	**8** Tamuz 22 1214 1184	**9** Tamuz 23 1215 1185	**10** Tamuz 24 1216 1186	**11** Tamuz 25 1217 1187
12 Tamuz 26 1218 1188	**13** Tamuz 27 1219 1189	**14** Tamuz 28 1220 1190	**15** Tamuz 29 1221 1191	**16** Av 1 1222 1192	**17** Av 2 1223 1193	**18** Av 3 1224 1194
19 Av 4 1225 1195	**20** Av 5 1226 1196	**21** Av 6 1227 1197	**22** Av 7 1228 1198	**23** Av 8 1229 1199	**24** Av 9 1230 1200	**25** Av 10 1231 1201
26 Av 11 1232 1202	**27** Av 12 1233 1203	**28** Av 13 1234 1204	**29** Av 14 1235 1205	**30** Av 15 1236 1206	**31** Av 16 1237 1207	

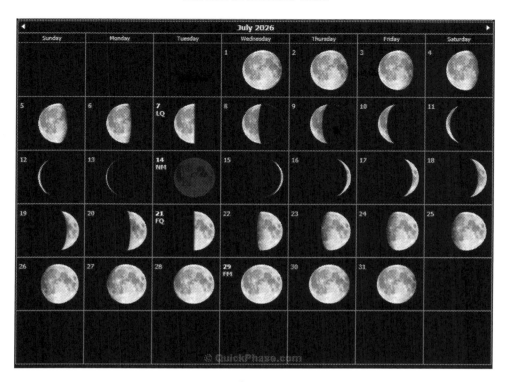

July 2026

August 2026 (Jewish Year 5786)						
Sunday	Monday	Tuesday	Wednesday	Thursday	Friday	Saturday
August 14: Av 30 ends at sunset (6:28 p.m.) and starts Elul 1. Elul is the sixth month of the Jewish calendar and has twenty-nine days.						**1** Av 17 1238 1208
2 Av 18 1239 1209	**3** Av 19 1240 1210	**4** Av 20 1241 1211	**5** Av 21 1242 1212	**6** Av 22 1243 1213	**7** Av 23 1244 1214	**8** Av 24 1245 1215
9 Av 25 1246 1216	**10** Av 26 1247 1217	**11** Av 27 1248 1218	**12** Av 28 1249 1219	**13** Av 29 1250 1220	**14** Av 30 1251 1221	**15** Elul 1 1252 1222
16 Elul 2 1253 1223	**17** Elul 3 1254 1224	**18** Elul 4 1255 1225	**19** Elul 5 1256 1226	**20** Elul 6 1257 1227	**21** Elul 7 1258 1228	**22** Elul 8 1259 1229
23 Elul 9 1260 1230	**24** Elul 10 1261 1231	**25** Elul 11 1262 1232	**26** Elul 12 1263 1233	**27** Elul 13 1264 1234	**28** Elul 14 1265 1235	**29** Elul 15 1266 1236
30 Elul 16 1267 1237	**31** Elul 17 1268 1238					

August 2026

September 2026 (Jewish Year 5786/5787)						
Sunday	Monday	Tuesday	Wednesday	Thursday	Friday	Saturday
September 22: Yom Kippur, the Day of Atonement.		1 Elul 18 1269 1239	2 Elul 19 1270 1240	3 Elul 20 1271 1241	4 Elul 21 1272 1242	5 Elul 22 1273 1243
6 Elul 23 1274 1244	7 Elul 24 1275 1245	8 Elul 25 1276 1246	9 Elul 26 1277 1247	10 Elul 27 1278 1248	11 Elul 28 1279 1249	12 Elul 29 1280 1250
13 Tishri 1 1281 1251	14 Tishri 2 1282 1252	15 Tishri 3 1283 1253	16 Tishri 4 1284 1254	17 Tishri 5 1285 1255	18 Tishri 6 1286 1256	19 Tishri 7 1287 1257
20 Tishri 8 1288 1258	21 Tishri 9 1289 1259	22 Tishri 10 JD 2461306 1290 1260	23 Tishri 11	24 Tishri 12	25 Tishri 13	26 Tishri 14
27 Tishri 15	28 Tishri 16	29 Tishri 17	30 Tishri 18	*September 22*: Christ's second coming—the Battle of Armageddon.		

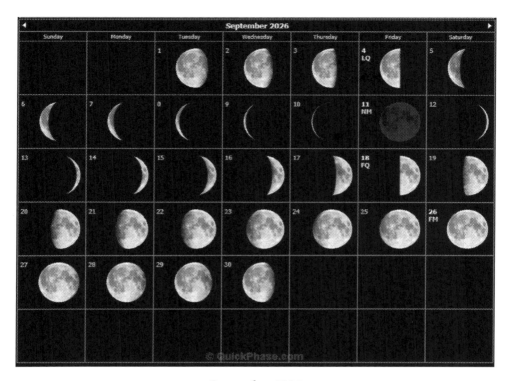

September 2026

September 12: Elul 29 ends at sunset (5:52 p.m.) and starts Tishri 1.

September 13: Tishri 1 ends at sunset. Tishri is the seventh month of the Jewish religious calendar and has thirty days.

September 22 (Tishri 10, 5787): This day is Yom Kippur, the appointed time called the Day of Atonement. This day is 2,550 days after the signing of the agreement with Israel. This day will start eternity. On this day, that which was spoken by Jude, the brother of James and servant of Jesus Christ and the apostle John, comes to fulfillment.

> "And Enoch also, the seventh from Adam, prophesied of these, saying, Behold, the Lord cometh with ten thousands of his saints, To execute judgment upon all, and to convince all that are ungodly among them of all

their ungodly deeds which they have ungodly committed, and of all their hard *speeches* which ungodly sinners have spoken against him. These are murmurers, complainers, walking after their own lusts; and their mouth speaketh great swelling *words*, having men's persons in admiration because of advantage. (Jude 1:14–16)

How that they told you there should be mockers in the last time, who should walk after their own ungodly lusts." (Jude 1:18)

And I saw heaven opened, and behold a white horse; and he that sat upon him *was* called Faithful and True, and in righteousness he doth judge and make war. His eyes *were* as a flame of fire, and on his head *were* many crowns; and he had a name written, that no man knew, but he himself. And he *was* clothed with a vesture dipped in blood: and his name is called The Word of God. And the armies *which were* in heaven followed him upon white horses, clothed in fine linen, white and clean. And out of his mouth goeth a sharp sword, that with it he should smite the nations: and he shall rule them with a rod of iron: and he treadeth the winepress of the fierceness and wrath of Almighty God. And he hath on *his* vesture and on his thigh a name written, KING OF KINGS, AND LORD OF LORDS. (Rev. 19: 11–16)

And I saw the beast, and the kings of the earth, and their armies, gathered together to make war against him that sat on the horse, and against his army. And the beast was taken, and with him the false prophet that wrought miracles before him, with which he deceived them that had received the mark of the beast, and them that worshipped his image. These both were cast alive into a lake of fire burning with brimstone. And the remnant were slain with the sword of him that sat upon the horse, which *sword* proceeded out of his mouth: and all the fowls were filled with their flesh." (Rev. 19: 19–21)

This final day will start a thousand-year reign by the Lord Jesus Christ. Following the thousand-year reign will be the White Throne judgment, when everyone who is not written in the book of life will be cast into the lake of fire.

Satan and his demons will be judged and cast there as well. The earth will pass away. God will create a new earth and bring down the New Jerusalem for those who have accepted His offer of eternal life. The city of New Jerusalem will be one thousand five hundred miles in length, width, and height.

Printed in the United States
By Bookmasters